HONJOK

Vivida

Vivida® is a trademark property of White Star s.r.l.
www.vividabooks.com

Piazzale Luigi Cadorna, 6
20123 Milan, Italy
www.whitestar.it

This edition first published in 2024 by

Om Books International

Corporate & Editorial Office
A-12, Sector 64, Noida 201 301
Uttar Pradesh, India
Phone: +91 120 477 4100
Email: editorial@ombooks.com
Website: www.ombooksinternational.com

Sales Office
107, Ansari Road, Darya Ganj,
New Delhi 110 002, India
Phone: +91 11 4000 9000
Email: sales@ombooks.com
Website: www.ombooks.com

ISBN: 9789353769703

Printed in India

10 9 8 7 6 5 4 3 2 1

SILVIA LAZZARIS

with Jade Jeongso An

HONJOK

The South Korean method of living happily with ourselves

Illustrations by
Giovanna Ferraris
Francesca Leoneschi

Om Books International

CONTENTS

Compared to other countries, modern South Korea views solitude perhaps in a slightly different way. For young Koreans, time spent alone is an opportunity to free ourselves, transform, and create work opportunities. Solitude represents our direction toward the future.

In the last fifty years, South Korea has undergone significant social and economic changes, often guided by technological advances. As technology progresses in society, young Koreans increasingly embrace a movement called *honjok*, the combination of *hon* (alone) and *jok* (tribe). A tribe of one. This movement is often called *naholojok*, which is comprised of *na* (myself), *holo* (alone) and *jok* (tribe). A tribe of myself, alone. These words are used interchangeably to describe people who decide to celebrate their solitude and independence by doing things by themselves: eating, drinking, watching a film, traveling, and just having fun.

Many other terms surround this solitary life choice. There are, for example, specific words that describe various activities that are carried out alone, such as eating (*honbap*), drinking (*honsul*), traveling (*honhaeng*), watching a film (*honyeong*), and shopping (*honsho*).

It's difficult to establish precisely when the concept *honjok* first appeared in South Korea, but an analysis by Daumsoft (one of the most widespread search engines in Korea) has shown that use of terms like *honbap*, *honsul*, and *honnol* exploded after 2010, going from 44 total citations at the beginning of the decade to over 60,000 in 2016. In the same period, the rate of smartphone ownership in South Korea increased from 14% to over 85%, due to a new type of consumer culture facilitated by social media. If on one hand personal technology like smartphones played an important role in elevating *honjok* to national status, on the other it may also reveal how South Koreans were attempting to escape physically and materially from Korea.

As a Millennial born and raised in Korea, but now living in Berlin, I often ask myself questions like: If I have fun eating and traveling alone, then am I, too, *honjok*? It must have been during my last year at university, between 2015 and 2016, when I started hearing the words *honjok* and *honbap* among friends on social media. In the same period, I also heard of *mukbang* (gastronomic spectacles in which people film themselves while eating). My friends told me that when they ate alone, they enjoyed watching other people, normally YouTubers, eat alone too.

At the time, it all seemed so bizarre to me, given that Korean culture is based on sharing food, which is consumed in families or among friends. Until recently, for example, students eating lunch alone in the school cafeteria would often feel stressed. They were concerned about appearing as loners. My friends said that eating alone without having to think about others was in a certain way liberating, an emancipation.

People who do things alone have understood that solitude doesn't necessarily mean loneliness. It makes us feel independent, adventurous, and, in the end, ourselves. Still, not all Koreans agree, above all the older generations, for whom solidarity has much more value than individualism. They're concerned about the choices of young *honjoks*, and they criticize their behavior as too independent and individualist.

To understand this phenomenon more thoroughly, I've spoken with people of every generation and background—young adults, students, parents and singles with young or grown children, as well as older adults. Within this book are key concepts and *honjok* solutions to make the most of spending time alone. This movement contains advice that all of us can learn, and that we can interpret as a method to live more effectively with ourselves.

Jade Jeongso An

Chapter 1

HONJOK

The Origins of *Honjok*

혼족의 기원

Why have many young South Koreans chosen an isolated lifestyle? The *honjok* movement is a new phenomenon and somewhat controversial. The word *honjok* began to spread throughout Korea with another expression, Hell Joseon—literally "Infernal Korea." This satirical expression, which began to circulate on the Internet in 2015, is used by young Koreans to express their disillusionment with the social and economic state of the country. Young Koreans, when complaining about youth unemployment and economic and social disparities, have engaged in a delightful activity: coining new words.

From birth, the youth hear that they must struggle to excel as students, workers, wives, husbands, mothers, and fathers. The perception is that, by tradition, there is only one way to be deserving citizens, which is often determined by one's social class at birth and how many private lessons their parents can afford. Discrimination is like a parasite for anyone who hasn't excelled in their studies and received a university degree from a prestigious institution, or for anyone who hasn't decided to start a family. Korean children learn all of this at a very young age. As author Euny Hong writes in her book *The Birth of Korean Cool*, if you waste your early years in Korea—childhood and adolescence—"you're finished, finished, finished." Some aspects of contemporary America are scandalous to Koreans, for example the idea that learning must be in some way fun.

Young *honjoks* have been raised in a collectivistic society. They haven't given themselves meaning; rather, they have built their identity based on the community they belong to and the role they've carried out within it. In collectivistic Korean culture, respect for authority is of utmost importance. Loyalty toward hierarchies is sacred, so much so that specific behavioral codes exist to speak with people of different ages and social classes. All actions are based on hierarchy. In her book, Hong points out that without knowing the age of the person you're speaking to, you don't know how to speak or behave. Social interaction is almost like an orchestra in which each person's roles change gradually as more instruments join in: each time someone enters a room, those present must recalibrate their behavior.

Honjok is born out of the desire to dismantle this system. In the last ten years, some young people have embraced *honjok* out of pleasure or practicality; others because they're exhausted. Many youths have retreated to the margins, minimizing their social interaction. They've embraced the concepts of "loner" or "loser," while at the same time making them cool. Being alone is an act of liberation. *Honjoks*, above all, live alone. And they even go out alone to dinner and the movies, or travel, play, sing, or shop alone. Some of them reject marriage, procreation, and even sex. Others do not. Some have simply reduced their sphere of friends, while others have almost completely isolated themselves. In the beginning, everyone did it more or less on their own. Then, thanks to a new term that became a viral hashtag, a bit like the success of the *#metoo* movement, they came together. In the span of a few years, thanks to the advent of new technologies and digital spaces, physical isolation has been

transformed into a virtual community of Instagrammers, YouTubers, members of apps and forums who have their own *koine* and share the same values. The Internet has transformed the invisibility and silence of outcasts into an increasingly forceful and loud voice.

In the eyes of many Koreans, *honjoks* aren't fighting to change society: they're egotistically renouncing the efforts required to make a change while only looking out for themselves. To them, however, living in solitude in order to find oneself is a revolutionary act. Despite the skeptics, *honjoks* have influenced the Korean economy and culture—and perhaps soon even in the West—and have won their first victories, like single-sized portions and products and the official recognition of the single-person family. But the most important victory has been psychological: isolation has spurred them to discover that peace can be found in solitude, that they don't need others' approval to feel in harmony with themselves, and that being alone doesn't necessarily mean feeling alone.

From those who practice *honjok* we can learn to view and appreciate solitude from another perspective. In the words of Honoré de Balzac, "Solitude is a beautiful thing; but it requires that someone else tell you that solitude is a beautiful thing." This is what *honjok* tells us. And not only that: this phenomenon can help us to recognize social pressures that we feel and can aid us in our personal emancipation. Perhaps some of us will never feel the same urgency to isolate ourselves as young Koreans. Some probably despise the very thought of having to entertain ourselves alone. But if we convince ourselves that there is nothing wrong with spending a Saturday night alone on the sofa, that there is no sadness in traveling alone to new destinations, and that deciding to be single is nothing strange, then the lessons of this movement will be useful to us too.

GLOS

Chosiknam, **초식남**: Literally "man-herbivores," "grass-eating men," it is borrowed from the Japanese to describe men who are not interested in marrying or having a lasting, serious relationship.

Geon-eo-mul-nyeo, **건어물녀**: It has the same meaning as *chosiknam*, but it refers to women instead.

Hikikomori, **히키코모리**: *Hikikomori* are defined as modern-day hermits. It is a Japanese term that refers to adults who retreat from society and voluntarily seek out extreme isolation.

Honbap, **혼밥**: *Bap* means "rice" in Korean. *Honbap* means "eating alone."

Honhaeng, **혼행**: *Haeng* is an abbreviation of *Yeo-haeng*, "travel." *Honhaeng* means "traveling alone."

Honjok, **혼족**: *Honjok* is the combination of two words: *hon* and *jok*. *Hon* means "alone" and *jok* means "tribe." It is a term used to designate people who willingly choose to live alone and to carry out activities alone, such as eating, watching a film, drinking, or shopping.

SARY

Honnol, 혼놀: *Nol* comes from *nol-da*, which means "play." *Honnol* means "play," "go out and spend time alone."

Honsho, 혼쇼: *Sho* derives from the English word "shopping." *Honsho* refers to shopping alone.

Honsul, 혼술: *Sul*, in Korean, means "alcohol." *Honsul* means "drinking alone."

Honyeong, 혼영: *Yeong* derives from *yeoung-hwa*, "film." *Honyeong* means "watching a film alone."

Naholojok, 나홀로족: This word has the same meaning as *honjok*. It is comprised of *na*, which means "myself," *holo* "alone," and *jok* "tribe." This is the term that is most widespread in Korea.

Chapter 1

1.1 Single-Person Families

1인가구

HONJOK

1인가구

In South Korea, family has been defined for centuries as "from birth and from economic cooperation under the same roof." The classic family was centered on marriage and the birth of children (especially males). Bringing children into the world was considered so important that, during the Joseon dynasty, the inability to procreate was seen as a sin to atone for.

It's not surprising that those who lived alone in the past were almost looked on with suspicion: if they're alone, then they must have a problem! Still today, the older generation often assumes that anyone who lives alone is in a period of transition. In modern Korea, however, single-person families are accepted more and more and recognized as having made a permanent choice. In the 1990s, this family typology composed one tenth of all nuclear families. Today, just twenty-five years later, more than one third of Korean families are *honjok*; in Seoul, it's almost fifty percent.

Living alone and without children often implies economic wellbeing. Many firms have understood this, giving rise to a new economy: the *hon-conomy*. In online shopping, *honjok* is listed as a separate category, where multi-purpose furniture can be found, kitchenware for one person, and mini washing machines. Supermarkets offer special deals on single-portion products, and the first restaurants and bars have emerged with single-seating tables with plexiglass dividers between customers. Cinemas have even begun to install single-seating halls. Personalizing every aspect of their life, *honjoks* gradually build a custom-made world around themselves, in which only people and objects that please them can enter. Everything else remains outside.

Chapter 1

1.2 Alone, but Connected

혼자지만 가끔 함께가 되는

I would daresay that a *honjok* lifestyle would be impossible without technology. Nowadays, between videocalls and remote work, interacting with other people is less a necessity and more a matter of choice. In recent years, the Korean economy has boosted e-commerce, and the government has invested in technologies that have made physical contact obsolete by incentivizing remote work, driverless cars, drones, and robots. So, is technology the cause or the solution for young Koreans' solitude? Maybe it's a bit of both.

If, on the one hand, living alone and staying glued to a phone may make us increasingly isolated, on the other, new digital tools can help us socialize in new ways. Rather than staying locked in their rooms and wondering what is wrong with themselves, *honjoks* have formed their identity and built a new community. On sites and apps like Honjok Dot Com and King of Honjok, users suggest restaurants and products, they share objects and organize events in which (occasionally, if they so desire) they can meet in person. Comments on vloggers' and YouTubers' pages are a place where the ideas, emotions, and frustrations of the hermit lifestyle can be shared.

Who said that it's necessary to meet in person to create genuine relationships and connect with others? The *honjok* approach can teach us how to refine our virtual social competencies. For example, we might try to identify a person's emotions by their voice inflections or tone of voice, or from the combination of pixels that make up their face. We might even attempt to get to know a person by their word choice or their use of punctuation. The important thing is to stay curious about others: in this way, every detail can tell a story.

Chapter 1

1.3 The Gaze of Others

타인의 시선

타인의 시선

Honjoks very often justify their life choice by stating that they prefer to do things "far from the gaze of others." They're referring to that look that can be interpreted as an intrusion, that makes us feel bad about ourselves. Young Koreans have just coined a new term to describe precisely this sort of violation: "gaze rape," literally "rape with your eyes."

The ways in which others look at us can limit our freedom in various ways, and *honjoks* have understood this. When someone looks too closely at how we're dressed, how we speak, or how we laugh, their gaze can make us feel judged and ashamed. Staring can make us feel vulnerable. Then there's that desire for approval that we seek in the eyes of others, to find in them the confirmation of our qualities or the validity of our choices. Even these gazes limit our freedom in a certain way: when we receive the desired positive feedback, sometimes we end up modifying our behavior until it corresponds with others' expectations.

Young *honjoks* are increasingly aware of the amount of energy that is invested each day in concerning ourselves with how others perceive us. Far from stranger's eyes, they feel liberated. This is why they decide to go and sing karaoke alone, or to take their own time finishing a meal alone. Alone in their homes, young Koreans can sing at the top of their lungs or dance carefree without any sort of embarrassment. An example of a recent victory are the "emotional empathy" services: at the entrances of certain Korean stores, one can find *honsho* stickers, which customers can wear in case they don't want to be disturbed by the clerks.

Chapter 1

1.4 Female Liberation

여성해방

HONJOK

Unmarried women in Korea are normally referred to as *mi-hon*. But in recent years, a new term—with a similar meaning, but profoundly different—has made its way into the language. The neologism *bi-hon* doesn't describe unmarried women who desire to be married, but rather those women who have made a conscious choice to remain single, who have no intention of getting married and aren't even convinced that they want to have children. Another neologism, a synonym of *bi-hon*, is *honyeo*: literally "solitary women" who live alone and have chosen a different pathway from the traditional one. These women would tell us: we respect the fact that for some people, marriage is a value, an ambition, a strength; but we believe that marriage isn't fundamental to our happiness, that no one has a right to impose on us.

It's not by chance that many *honjoks* are women. In South Korea, a young woman who lives alone is a revolutionary. Being *bi-hon* is a way to place one's individual needs and desires not necessarily above emotions, insofar as marriage is an institution which in Korea represents traditional loyalty to hierarchy and authority. *Bi-hon* women repudiate a cultural system that relegates them to a sole function in society, that of wives and mothers. According to *bi-hon* women, Korean society tends to disparage women who at thirty years of age are not married with children. They have reclaimed certain terms and given them new meanings, positive ones, ones that reflect their lifestyle.

Being *bi-hon* means making an unconventional choice, but above all it means not doing so in silence. It might mean taking part in the *#nomarriage* or the *#EMIF* movement (Elite without Marriage, I am going Forward). But above all it means letting other women know, regardless of the choices they make, that we will not judge them.

Chapter 1

1.5 The *Honjok* Home

혼족의 주거실태

For *honjoks,* it isn't difficult to build a nest fit for a single. The Korean government has introduced a loan system to help the growing number of single-person families. Through a subsidy scheme, the state issues a credit card, and you can borrow the required amount of money necessary to establish your home. Alternatively, the government makes available small apartments in buildings with common spaces like a garden or gym. They are inexpensive, geared toward increasing sociability among singles in a sort of college-dorm experience.

Living alone in a large house is too difficult to manage and too costly. In minuscule one or two-room apartments, beauty, order, and efficiency take on vital importance for *honjoks*. "Effort" and "diligence" are the most prevalent words that *honjoks* use to speak about the commitment that it takes to keep a small space organized. Television series that provide advice to *honjoks* on how to manage their budget to furnish their home have become increasingly popular. An entire economy has emerged around mini-refrigerators and mini-washing machines, tools for vacuum-sealing food packages to make them last longer, beds that double as sofas or desks.

The homes that *honjoks* show with pride online all look very similar. They have very few objects and are super-organized. The message seems to be: If you have no intention of wearing a shirt more than once a week, then it has no place in the house. If you don't have boxes and racks to organize your clothes by color, you're destined to live in chaos. If you decide to put a dark-colored piece of furniture somewhere, you'd better have a good explanation for it.

Chapter 1

1.6 Behind the Screen

컴퓨터 스크린 앞에서

Honjoks and I watch the same TV shows. When I spoke with some of them, I discovered that they spend a lot of time watching Netflix, but watching foreign TV series doesn't have the same meaning for me as it does for them. If European culture has been influenced for decades by foreign cinema, especially American, foreign cultural artifacts have only been present in Korea for about the last twenty years. The Korean government feared a cultural colonization from countries like Japan and America and was shocked by the direct and obscene nature of certain films or the lyrics of some songs.

I try to imagine what it means to be the first generation to be exposed to foreign cultural influences. If spending too much time in front of the television can seem like a waste of time in Western culture, for *honjoks* watching TV is a way to feel in touch with world history. Proximity to other cultures through television also implies idealizing the lives of those who live worlds away. Eun-Kyoung is a *honjok* girl who, like me, loves watching "Modern Family", an American series based on the ups and downs of a large family whose members all live in a suburb of Los Angeles. I told Eun-Kyoung that I feel homesick when I watch the program. She paused. It doesn't have the same effect on her: she knows her family would never be as close as the one in the series. As someone who assiduously visits streaming sites, Eun-Kyoung has developed, like many *honjoks*, an emotional defense mechanism. Watching television is entertainment, but it doesn't create in her unattainable expectations in real life.

Chapter 1

1.7 Facing Solitude

외로움,
극복 아닌
공존하기

It's easy to imagine *honjoks* as introverts, aloof, who take no pleasure in being with others. Describing them in this way would mean relegating them to a stereotype. It's true that the majority of *honjoks* have fun without needing anyone around them, find pleasure in doing things alone. But many young Koreans who live alone have friends they're often in contact with and whom they see occasionally, and they don't disdain the company of others.

Being *honjok* doesn't imply being immune to loneliness—it means, on the contrary, being exposed to it on a regular basis, and therefore perhaps also learning how to manage it with more thoughtfulness. An article on Honjok Dot Com describes how the advantages of living alone sometimes fall short of avoiding a sense of loneliness. The article describes this feeling as entirely natural: we all feel lonesome at times, the site states, but overcoming this feeling with wisdom is important. All it takes is a series of wise strategies to prevent and manage loneliness.

Don't disconnect your space from the outside world

Living alone, we run the risk of being trapped in our world. At times, our custom-made world can seem entertaining and fulfilling; but over time, this personal space can be filled with anxiety and regret. This is why we should try to keep our curtains open and let the light in, open the door regularly and let the air come through. Hearing the sounds and smelling the scents of the outside world, just as observing what is going on outside our home, can help us to remember three important things: that we are not alone in the world; that the world doesn't revolve around us; and that we, too, are a part of something.

Understand precisely what causes loneliness

In psychological research, loneliness is often broken down into social loneliness and emotional loneliness: social loneliness means having a smaller group of loved ones around us than we would otherwise desire, and emotional loneliness means having less-intense relationships than we desire. In both cases, the loneliness lies in the discrepancy between what one wants and what one has. In order to overcome loneliness, we must understand our unfulfilled needs when we feel lonely. Perhaps it's returning to an empty home and having no one to talk to about our day? Once the problem is clear, we can then take action: in our example, the solution could be to call a friend or a member of our family when we come home, or invite them to dinner.

Accentuate the joy of living alone

Waking up alone every morning could make us feel lonesome—but also free and independent if we appreciate those activities we can carry out without shame when living alone. Dancing in our underwear in the kitchen and singing in the shower are two trivial examples. We should seek out activities of this sort—invisible to others, but liberating for us—and try to practice them every day, particularly when we feel alone.

Cuddle with a pet

Pets are suggested as a cure for loneliness. With pets, we can not only communicate, but even share our feelings. Pets provide a stable presence and show gratitude and affection. The suggestion is not only for cats and dogs: even tropical fish, parrots, and other small animals can live and interact with us and among themselves. Observing them and taking care of them, we feel less lonely.

Try something new

It's difficult to feel alone when we learn a new skill. One of the best ways to prevent solitude would be to increase the time we feel creative, challenged, and enriched. This is more a way to prevent loneliness than to cure it: if we feel desperate and lonely, we may not even have the strength or the will to try new things. If we realize that we don't have the strength to manage our inner loneliness, we know that the time is right to entrust ourselves to others.

Have fun with others

In order to live alone peacefully, we need to fill our home with close friends every now and then. It doesn't have to be a luxurious evening or a grand event: all it takes is getting together, drinking something, chatting and laughing. And when we can't get together, it's important to stay in touch in other ways: a videocall while cooking or eating, or spending an evening together playing online. Despite the fact that the suggestion to surround yourself with friends is listed in last place, the article on Honjok Dot Com affirms that it is the best way to live alone without feeling lonely. Far from the stereotype, the best antidote against loneliness—even for *honjoks* is—friendship.

Chapter 1

1.8 Surrogate Partners

가상 파트너

HONJOK

가상 파트너

Coming home and finding no one there, or falling asleep and waking up in the same bed alone, can be difficult over time and make us depressed. For this reason, in South Korea and other Asian countries in which increasing number of people who choose to live alone, a new market is developing around products geared toward emotional comfort. There is hope that these products can take the place of certain functions that have customarily been carried out by flesh-and-blood partners.

Azuma Hikari, for example, is a digital partner that appears as a hologram inside a Gate Box, a box that looks like a coffee maker or a blender. She was created by a Japanese company and will be available for sale in 2021, but some *honjoks* have already had a chance to try her. Azuma is twenty years old and has blue hair. She says "good morning" and, thanks to various sensors and artificial intelligence software, she is able to recognize your voice and face. As you prepare to leave the house, she speaks to you about the weather and, given that she can even sync with your agenda, she reminds you to leave the house if you're running late. During the day, you can exchange messages—and if you tell her you're on your way home, this seems to make her happy. Azuma stays awake with you until you fall asleep.

There's also the pillow partner. One of the feelings that is most missed by *honjok* girls is falling asleep in a partner's arms. In order to recreate the same sensation, a Chinese company has developed an arm and a chest. *Honjok* girls can purchase different types of arms of partners: thin and traditional partners that wear a pajama sleeve, or partners with tan and muscular arms that "sleep" with a bare chest.

Chapter 1

1.9 Pacing Oneself

나의 시간은 나의 자유

HONJOK

Young *honjoks* think they have something that many others in their age group don't: time. The Korean writer Park Hong-Soon believed that the growing quantity of superfluous objects and information in our lives causes mental and bodily fatigue, as well as strain within our space. With regard to such excess, Hong-Soon views the *honjok* lifestyle as a relaxation of the mind and the body. *Honjoks* simplify and reduce external impulses in order to dedicate themselves to introspection. For young Koreans, slowness is not a question of personal inclination; it is a lifestyle choice. In a frenetic and competitive society, *honjoks* get by with reduced external space, which becomes a vast interior space, because it is there that they decide how much time they have at their disposal, how to utilize it, and in what ways to be stimulated.

To some people, this choice may appear disobedient, even anti-patriotic. To others, it seems necessary, because it is sustainable and respectful not of one nation, but of a global, interconnected community that shares the planet. Different *honjok* blogs speak of the necessity of singling out what is really necessary and what activities and objects add value to our lives, and of leaving the rest out. Living like a *honjok* means being more frugal and reflecting on true needs—our own, as well as those of the planet. Even if living more simply can have different meanings for different people, according to *honjoks* at least two results of this lifestyle are the same for everyone: Eliminating disorder from our pathway enables us to provoke less environmental and social damage, but also to have more time, which implies more freedom, in order to find the true meaning that we want to give to our existence.

The RANGE of HONJOKS

Despite the fact that the term *honjok* refers to people who live and prefer to do things alone, *honjoks* can have different types of personality, and not all of them are necessarily introverted. Just because a person likes to eat alone rather than with other people, does this make her the same type of *honjok* as someone who loves to eat with others, but to travel alone? The spectrum of introversion-extroversion can be applied, as with all people, even to *honjoks*.

Despite the fact that these terms can help us to recognize difference among the various ways of socializing, we must remember, that reality is much more diverse and complex than these three simple categories.

 BY JADE JEONGSO AN

INTROVERTED *HONJOK*

If you prefer above all to spend time alone, and prefer to do activities autonomously rather than socially, you're probably an introverted *honjok*. Introverted *honjoks* feel recharged after doing things alone. Although they feel assured of the things they do alone, they might feel embarrassed or timid about what others think of them. For example, they would never eat alone in famous restaurants that require at least a one-hour wait in line. They prefer to buy something from the drive-through and eat it in the car.

AMBIVERTED *HONJOK*

If sometimes you feel introverted and other times extroverted, and you can go from one to the other depending on the circumstances, then perhaps you have something in common with the "ambiverted" *honjok*. They like to spend time with others, but they definitely need time to themselves. The typical ambiverted *honjok* loves free time, reading or watching a film alone, but prefers to carry out other activities with others, such as traveling.

EXTROVERTED *HONJOK*

If you're not ashamed to do things alone, and you appreciate the time you spend alone as much as the time you spend with others, then you resemble the extroverted *honjok*. *Honjoks* that belong to this category are easygoing, pleasant, and outgoing because they enjoy others' company. These are the *honjoks* that travel abroad, sleep in hostels to make new friends, and eat alone in foreign restaurants while exchanging small talk with the wait staff.

Types of

*   **   ***   ****

The philosopher (introvert) *

You, too, are the philosopher type if you prefer introspection over many other activities. *Honjoks* who belong to this group are more outgoing toward people they've already cultivated a relationship with. Their preferred way of spending time is to dedicate themselves, alone, to activities that make them happy. They love going to museums or the movies alone. Although they feel more at ease alone, eating in public alone would make them feel embarrassed. You can often see them picking up their dinner from a take-away restaurant.

The minimalist (introvert, ambivert) **

Are you concerned about the fate of the environment, the economy? Do you think twice before purchasing "buy one, get two" objects? You might belong to the category of minimalists who commit themselves to living thoughtfully and with little. Minimalist *honjoks* prefer to eat alone in a school cafeteria or a company restaurant because they're more economical. They also actively look for products geared toward single-person families in order to reduce costs and waste. They're not particularly interested in traveling, and they go to restaurants with others in order to share the expense and save money.

The independent (antisocial, extrovert) ***

Don't judge independent types harshly just because they love to socialize. They can be extroverted and loud in some circumstances, but secretly they love to eat alone at home while watching their favorite TV programs. They even like the idea of traveling alone, and occasionally they try to organize trips of this sort; but every time they try, they end up inviting their friends: they'll have fun with them, but they'll also feel exhausted, anticipating their return home to take a warm bath alone.

The YOLO, "You only live once" (extrovert) ****

The acronym "YOLO" comes from Internet slang and became widespread in youth music and culture around 2010. It means living life to its fullest without regrets and sometimes taking risks. YOLO can describe one *honjok* personality type, and the YOLO lifestyle is based on doing things for oneself and alone. *Honjoks* in this category live a luxurious single lifestyle, sharing their daily activities publicly and investing in food, travel, and even pets. Typical YOLOs have one or two hobbies that keep them occupied every day, they have no partner, and they have lived or traveled abroad.

A DAY *in the* LIFE *of* Eun-Kyung Jeong

29, woman, YOLO

Eun-Kyung lives alone with her four-legged friend Sun-Duk. She begins her day with a morning walk with her dog. She returns home, has her breakfast, and gets ready for work. After a long day of work, her desire would be to return home and cook a delicious meal, following recipes on her favorite blogs and watch Netflix or Whatcha. But not always does it work out this way, and Eun-Kyung often ends up making a simple meal because she gets home late from the office.

BY JADE JEONGSO AN

Cooking for herself is a challenge for Eun-Kyung, in part because she tries to buy local products in traditional markets in Korea in which food is often sold in large quantities, but at the same time she needs food for a single-person family. When she manages to cook dinner, she first takes a look at streaming programs, thinking about what to watch while she eats. She often decides to watch *Mukbang*, a show that highlights other people eating in front of a television camera, because she saves her favorite programs for when she goes to bed. After dinner, she takes another stroll with SunDuk. After that, she cuddles again with him and gets ready for bed, where she'll watch a film or an episode of a TV series before falling asleep.

Sometimes Eun-Kyung begins her day at the beach, where she takes surf lessons, and then carries on as usual to go to work, where lunch is the only time in the week at which she eats with other people.

The weekend is not particularly different from other workdays: she has a bit more time to go out with SunDuk, taking him on some walks or along the beach. Weekend days are important for her, because she can dedicate time to arts and hobbies like sewing, working, and knitting—or even to moving the furniture in her small house to try new layouts. As long as she has things to do alone (and with her dog), she never has time to get bored.

Chapter 2

HONBAP

Solitary Meals

혼밥

HONBAP

혼자하는 식사

In Korea, people who live alone eat approximately half of their meals in solitude. *Honjoks* have a specific term to indicate eating alone: *honbap*. This neologism is the combination of *hon* (alone) and *bap* (rice, which in Korean generally means "food"). In Korea, food is a way not only to forge ties, but also to define social roles—both in the family and in public. For this reason, sitting at table remains one of the many situations that reveal the inequalities rooted in society, and the table itself has become another context in which the generational and social confrontation of *honjoks* plays out. Young *honbaps*, while eating alone, separate themselves from the imposition of a harsh label that is a part of the class system. At the same time, however, they risk losing the positive aspects of the socialization of mealtime, on which the entire Korean culinary tradition rests.

In fact, fried eggs are the most popular meal for *honbaps*. The reason lies in the fact—according to a study conducted in Korea—that whereas, for people who eat with others, it would seem that equal importance is given to simplicity, familiarity, and the taste of food, for those who eat alone, simplicity is the only important aspect of eating. For *honbaps*, the taste of food is the least important part of a meal. In minuscule *honjok* homes, it is easier to prepare instant noodles or reheat a frozen pizza. Food is above all functional (and not even so healthful). This frightens the older Korean generation, who realize that many young Koreans will no longer be able to prepare typical Korean dishes. Is it possible that a thousand-year-old culinary tradition might fade into oblivion just because of a few generations who prefer to eat alone?

This phenomenon isn't taking root only in Korea. The American author Michael Pollan has written that "we are in a struggle with a system that seeks to destroy the food culture, that doesn't want us to eat with others, but rather alone, in our cars." Increasing numbers of adults eat alone, and more often even in other parts of the world. But eating with others is still somehow profoundly rooted in our collective global conscience, and eating alone is still seen as anomalous behavior in many countries, including South Korea. Even on this point, however, the world is polarized. For many people in many countries, "social eating" is the norm. On the one hand, there are those who believe that eating a meal alone is a highly undesirable situation; some would even go so far as to affirm that an opportunity to eat alone cannot even be defined as a meal (at most, a snack!). On the other hand, some people interpret solitary meals as an opportunity to flee from public control and avoid negative aspects of sociality.

The debate in Korea—and the world—on meals has intensified in recent years, when food-delivery apps, online streaming, and fast-food establishments have made eating alone more feasible and tolerable. But philosophers and writers have expressed their views on this topic for centuries. The Greek philosopher Epicurus, over two thousand years ago, considered eating alone an uncivil act. For him, dining alone was akin to living like a lion or a wolf.

Even the French philosopher Jean Baudrillard mentioned the animal world, to state that nothing would contradict the laws of the animal world more than a man who eats alone. According to Baudrillard, sharing or competing for food together is a distinguishing feature of animals. But there were supporters of the *honjok* meal even in antiquity. It seems that one day the Roman politician Lucullus decided to order a meal for himself because he was tired of eating in the company of others. But when the meal arrived, he realized that it hadn't been prepared following the classic standards of the banquet, and he complained to the cook. The cook replied that he didn't think it was necessary to devote much attention to food for a man who would eat alone, and Lucullus countered that it was precisely when Lucullus dined alone that the cook should pay particular attention to the quality of his meal. It's easy to see how *honbap* can be considered both an advantage and a loss, as in fact is the case for the entire *honjok* movement. As in every social and cultural transformation, it's probably a bit of both. In this case, however, given that *honbap* is not an isolated movement, but rather a global trend, it will be interesting to discover the ways in which young *honbaps* relate to food and learn to enjoy a meal alone without remorse or shame. Above all, however, observing the way in which Korea will attempt to reconcile the new *honbap* lifestyle with its ancient culinary tradition could be a reference point for other countries that might face the same generational crisis.

Chapter 2

2.1 From Kimchi to Panini

두레상에서 혼밥으로

HONBAP

The first foundational value of Korean cuisine is waiting. Koreans proudly say that, despite the term "slow food," which was coined in Italy, no country has more slow food than Korea, the homeland of fermented foods. The longer you wait, the better the Korean food. The most prized versions of soy sauce, for example, are aged over 60 years: a famous saying suggests preparing it when the mother is pregnant, in order to be able to consume it at the wedding of the child. Another important value is sharing. In restaurants, Koreans order a large dish to be shared, accompanied by banchan, small side dishes that look a bit like tapas. But even these minuscule portions are sometimes shared with others. Unlike in Western countries, in Korea no one would dare order food for himself alone.

The *honbap* lifestyle embraces both of these principles. Living alone means choosing what to eat autonomously, but it also means giving up the preparation and sharing of traditional dishes in Korean cuisine. The preparation of fermented foods like kimchi, for example, usually involves an entire family. Young *honbaps*, for reasons of space, time, and practicality, have so far preferred inexpensive and easily accessible dishes: instant noodles, rice with simple side dishes, sandwiches. Worried that the *honbap* lifestyle will disrupt a chain of traditions handed down for generations, Koreans are looking for solutions: for example, catering for singles and the sale of devices to cook small portions of typical dishes. According to some, the identity crisis of young *honbaps* will make Korean cuisine more accessible in both its preparations and portions—creating a more internationalized version that will conquer the rest of the world.

Chapter 2

2.2 A Table for One, Please

혼자 왔어요

혼자 왔어요

HONBAP

There is a saying in Korean: food eaten alone doesn't taste good. Owners and customers of *honbap* restaurants do not agree. The image that's most analogous to a *honbap* restaurant is that of an open-space office. Individual wooden tables that look like desks, and arranged in two columns facing the same direction, like on an airplane. The gaze of others is separated by dividers between one table and another, each one set up with a screen and an electric burner. That's right, because you can cook the food you want alone as you watch television, in a strange space halfway between public and private.

Upon entering any Korean restaurant, you'll hear the same question: "a table for how many?" If eating is sociality, chatting and sharing, a meal consumed alone is perceived as a sad event (if out of necessity) and even deplorable (if by choice). In *honbap* restaurants, however, the host will only suggest that you sit wherever you'd like.

Increasing numbers of young Koreans practice the *honbap* lifestyle. The results of a study published in 2019 by the Korea Health Promotion Institute have shown that most people who eat alone are between 20 and 30 years old. The main reasons for deciding to eat alone are the possibility of choosing the time and the menu of the meal, but also not having anyone with whom to eat or not having time for a lunch with others. In the eyes of a portion of the Korean population, solitary restaurants are pathetic places, full of losers with no friends who drown their solitude in fat. In the eyes of others, however, they are the sign of a noble evolution of Korean social culture that has discovered the senselessness of feeling ashamed for eating alone.

Chapter 2

2.3 An Exercise in Self-Confidence

혼밥 눈치 안 봐요

HONBAP

혼밥 눈치 안 봐요

In recent years, several celebrities have practiced *honbap* in front of a TV camera, whether on their own YouTube channels or on live national television. The approval of pop stars has generated interest for this new trend and made it increasingly acceptable in the eyes of young Koreans. The K-Pop star Tiffany Young, for example, in recent years has regularly published YouTube videos of herself having lunch or dinner alone. In one of her clips, titled "Tiffany eats ramen alone!", the singer is having fun describing *honbap* as a video game composed of nine levels, which seem to reflect the level of self-confidence it takes to eat alone in situations normally perceived by the Korean population as increasingly embarrassing.

Are we beginners, or professional *honbaps*?

Do we have problems eating alone in any of these circumstances?

1. Kimbap or ramen, at home or on the go, which can happen to many people.
2. In a small restaurant or a cafeteria, where eating alone is normal.
3. In a fast-food restaurant, where many people grab a quick bite alone.
4. In a café, where solitary customers seem increasingly rare.
5. In a Chinese restaurant, where it's difficult to find tables for one.
6. In famous or romantic restaurants, experiences that are normally shared with others.
7. In family-run restaurants, where too many questions might make us feel judged.
8. In restaurants offering Korean barbecues, frequented by groups of people.
9. In a pub, while drinking an alcoholic beverage, in which the judgment of others is always guaranteed.

Chapter 2

2.4 *Mukbang*

먹방

먹방

Another phenomenon began alongside the birth and spread of *honbap*. It's called *mukbang*: a neologism formed by the combination of the Korean words "eat" and "show." In fact, *mukbang* is a television show in which the host eats while speaking into the camera. Launched on Korean television in 2009, it arrived on YouTube in 2011. Since then, it has become trendy in Korea and other parts of the world (particularly in the United States).

In the beginning, *mukbang* meant eating shocking quantities of food in front of the television camera. The hosts earned thousands of dollars per meal in the form of donations from viewers, who incited them to satisfy peculiar requests in the chat—like chewing as loudly and messily as possible.

Over time, however, *mukbang* has evolved into a wider concept: besides serial hamburger eaters, other hosts have achieved fame preparing traditional Korean dishes and eating in a composed manner in front of the camera. My favorite *mukbang* creator, for example, is MommyTang. She can be seen eating noodles or preparing traditional Korean recipes, like kimchi, in a vegan style. Her channel has half a million viewers, and I'm not surprised. Watching her in such a simple and banal context, like moving around the kitchen, is at once intimate and hypnotic.

It's not by chance that *honbap* and *mukbang* were created at the same time. The sharing of meals is an important traditional Korean value, and many young people who live and eat alone make use of *mukbang* to recover a sense of belonging and sharing. Despite eating at home, the Internet has made it such that some hosts have become guests at the tables of millions of young Koreans.

Chapter 2

2.5 Farewell to Etiquette

굿바이 · 식사예절

HONBAP

It isn't easy to sit at a Korean table without making mistakes: the rules of proper etiquette are extremely rigid. According to some *honbaps*, behind such formality is often hidden a class-based pretension that makes anyone feel inadequate who doesn't know or practice the etiquette properly. Young Koreans, as they grow up, have learned the rules well—and now they take even more delight in breaking them. For *honbaps*, eating alone means freeing oneself of the strictures of traditional rules and the social inequalities they represent.

The rules to break:

Remember rank

When we join others at table, it is immediately necessary to try to identify a sort of social ranking: in families it might be based on age; at a business lunch, by title; with friends or acquaintances, by rank. Without any information that allows us to understand who are the more or less prestigious people among us, it would be impossible to understand when to begin to eat (the oldest person or highest-ranking person eats first), or where to sit (the youngest must sit closest to the door). *Honjoks* can avoid making any of these calculations, and when they enter a restaurant they can sit where they like and begin eating without too many pleasantries.

Follow the rhythm of others

When we eat in a group, it can happen that someone eats a bit too fast, and someone else too slow. In Korea, however, one must be particularly cognizant of eating at the same pace as others—who could feel offended by those who eat too fast (perhaps he or she wants to leave the table as soon as possible?) or by those who eat too slow (perhaps he or she didn't like the food?). Some Koreans believe that the ability to adapt one's pace to that of others has become a spontaneous act. Others, however, among whom are many *honbaps*, believe that only by eating alone can one regain his or her own natural rhythm.

Don't lift your plate

Unlike in many other Asian countries, in Korea it is considered rude to lift plates and bowls to finish the last grain of rice or drop of soup. Alone at home, far from the sneers of disapproval, *honbaps* can concentrate on avoiding waste.

Eat seated and in a closed space

Eating while on the go is another *honbap* joy. Until recently, for Koreans, strolling with an ice cream or a coffee in hand would have been thought of like walking down the street while sipping a pint of Guinness at the most improbable times of the day, is thought of now. Now that many people do it, this habit has become normalized, and no one is shocked anymore.

Honbap rules:

Don't let yourself be influenced by the wait staff

For *honbaps*, you don't have to be ashamed to eat alone. When you enter a restaurant and state that you'll be eating alone, you do so with your head held high, without the fear of being judged. A *honbap* lunch is an act of freedom.

Don't be afraid to request a table with a view

Just because you're eating alone, there's nothing that says you should hide in a corner of the restaurant!

Concentrate on the food, not on the people

The *honbap* approach to food is more aware and mindful than many others. Instead of eating and speaking at the same time, a *honbap* meal is a unique opportunity to enjoy food with all of your senses.

Bring a distraction, but don't be one yourself!

It's perfectly fine if you want to watch a film while eating; but if you're in a restaurant, you'll have to wear headphones or watch with subtitles to avoid disturbing the people around you.

At home, everything goes

Perhaps the most important rule for *honbaps* is that if your meals are eaten at home, everything goes: eating at the table, on the sofa, on the floor, in bed. Watching television, using your cell phone, listening to music while concentrating on the food. Fast, slow, or a combination of both. There are no rules in your personal space, in which food once again becomes a source of nourishment and ceases to fulfill its role as a social convention.

Chapter 2

2.6 Food Portions

1인분의 기준

As *honbaps* increase, food portions decrease. In order to satisfy the necessities of young *honbaps*, in fact, the size of portions must change. Small snacks for one person, usually sold in minimarkets and convenience stores, have had much success in recent years among young *honjoks*. Recently, however, many of them have begun to criticize such individual servings. The quantity of packaging (often in plastic) used does not justify the minuscule quantity of food they contain.

Besides seeking more sustainable choices, young Koreans are accustomed to healthy food, and many of them do not want to give in to fast-food culture and entirely give up cooking with fresh ingredients. "Meal kits" seem to be the new solution on the horizon. The kits are boxes that contain a series of recipes and all of the ingredients needed to prepare them. The boxes come in different sizes based on the number of people eating, and inside one can find fresh ingredients without packaging: for example, single cloves of garlic, a sprinkle of herbs, a handful of rice, and the precise number of vegetables needed for the recipe. This for *honbaps* is revolutionary: it means cooking for oneself without having to finish many superfluous and space-consuming leftovers in their minuscule refrigerators.

The request for increasingly smaller portions has spurred some Korean researchers to modify the genes of watermelons to make them single portions. The result is the "apple-watermelon": a watermelon the size of a golden apple with an edible rind. Since June 2020, this agricultural invention has begun to be exported to Singapore and Hong Kong with resounding success—who knows if one day it will arrive in your supermarket?

NUNCHI

In Korean culture, food is the center around which everything else revolves. Eating means eating together. Together with anyone—family, friends, colleagues, or any other group we're a part of—in order not to eat alone. A typical Korean meal is comprised of a bowl of rice, a main dish, a soup, and a series of side dishes called banchan—among which we can find the infamous kimchi. All food is shared. We Koreans always ask each other "Have you already eaten?" as if it were a way of asking how someone is feeling. Eating is a fundamental social activity, a daily activity in the life of Koreans. This is why the idea of eating alone is often synonymous with heightened embarrassment.

There is also another concept incorporated in the way Koreans think, which makes people reluctant to accept the *honbap* movement. It's called *nunchi*, which refers to being aware of others and the surrounding environment. *Nunchi* is like a sixth sense: it makes Koreans attentive to what people think and feel at any moment.

It is precisely for their sense of *nunchi* that makes sitting at table or entering a barbecue restaurant (usually frequented by groups) alone, difficult for Koreans. Some people feel shame and discomfort when dining alone in a restaurant. For others, even the thought of eating alone at home could be discouraging. Eating alone, however, has become the preferred activity of *honbaps*.

BY JADE JEONGSO AN

A MEAL AT SNOWFOX

Snowfox is one of the largest take-away restaurants in Seoul, whose mission is to offer top-quality fresh meals at an affordable price. Snowfox's menu includes hot dishes, salads, sushi, and sandwiches. This business was started without *honbaps* in mind, but its atmosphere and mission are making it a reference point for many young *honbaps*. I met with Hyunjoo Baek, CEO of Snowfox Korea, and discussed her customers, recent trends, and Snowfox's future.

"Snowfox has shelves full of healthful, ready-made fresh dishes. People don't need to wait for their order, which is the toughest part of eating in traditional restaurants. What's more, our restaurants offer a discreet and comfortable atmosphere, with individual tables and chairs, as well as rooms for large groups. Even people who want to eat alone feel comfortable in our restaurants. Most of our customers eat alone; I'm not sure if it's our setup or if it's because of the fact that our restaurant is becoming trendy in the *honbap* community. We didn't plan our business specifically for *honbaps*, but the culture of eating alone has slowly and naturally become a part of Korean culture, which has ensured our success.

"We want to offer healthy food that's easy to eat for as many people as possible. I think the trend of eating alone will grow. This is why it's important for us, as a reference

BY JADE JEONGSO AN

point for honbaps, to concentrate on using the freshest ingredients possible in order to prepare healthful and tasty food for our customers."

Types of

*

**

***

****

And you? How comfortable do you feel eating alone? On the basis of your level of ease in eating alone, you can place yourself in one of the following categories.

The neophyte *

If you enjoy spending Sunday afternoon alone in a café with a good cup of tea and a book, you could be a beginner *honbap*. You still feel a bit timid ordering a large meal to eat alone, but you can't give up drinking your coffee alone. If you happen to be a bit more comfortable, you could move on to pastry cookies. In order to fit into this category, it suffices to have breakfast alone in a café with a cappuccino and a chocolate croissant.

The efficient type **

We all know that in the modern world, with its frenetic rhythms, time is increasingly important. Efficient *honbaps* eat lunch alone in order to have more time during the day. This goes hand in hand with ordering (or going to buy) take-away food. Some honbaps in this category could, for example,

BY JADE JEONGSO AN

sit and eat at a fast-food counter or at a table in a café, surrounded by other people. Efficient *honbaps* are not influenced by the presence of others while they eat. If you're the classic efficient type, you could use your lunch break to concentrate entirely on yourself, learning new tricks—maybe even a new language!

The trendsetter ***

If you like to share the things you do on social media and discover the most promising places to visit, then you could be a trendsetter *honbap*. If you belong to this category, you don't mind exploring the latest trends alone—deep down, you prefer doing things alone to doing them with others. You're the only one in your group of friends willing to wait in line for two hours to get into that fashionable restaurant you saw on Instagram. At the end of your wait, you don't mind at all sitting at the table alone, concentrating on your food, and maybe even taking a picture to post on social media to share with your virtual friends.

"I want it, NOW!" ****

If food is a spontaneous act that has nothing to do with sociality, such that you would dine at a top restaurant alone, then you could be a professional *honbap*. You aren't ashamed to order as much food as you want and to eat it alone, even if surrounded by large groups that share their food and cast an occasional sneer at you. For you, there are no snacks or serious meals, no first-class or second-class foods. If you want to eat something in particular, even an expensive food, you do it without thinking twice, and you don't need to wait for the moment to share a meal with other people.

Between SOLITUDE *and* COMPANY

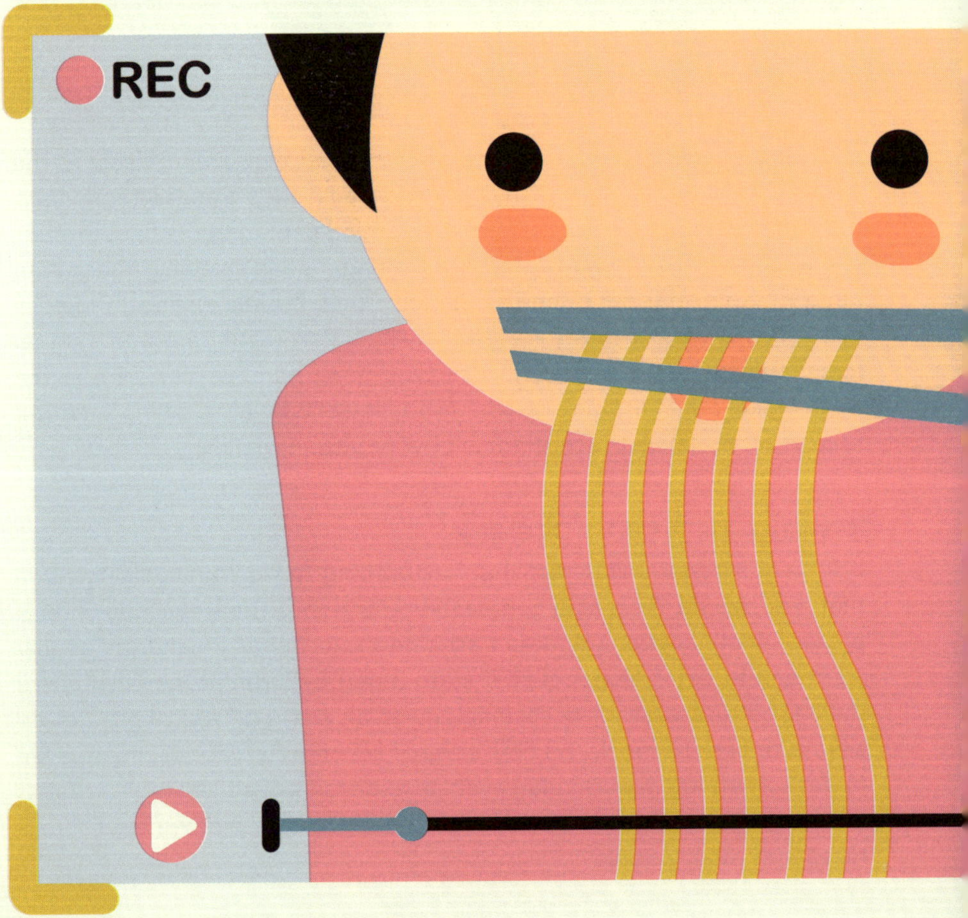

BY JADE JEONGSO AN

If you asked a *honjok* what five things they couldn't do without, streaming would surely be one of them, whether YouTube, Twitch, Netflix, Whatcha, Amazon Prime, or others. If you asked the same question to a *honbap*, they would answer even more unequivocally: any streaming platform that shows people eating—that is, *mukbang*. Why has *mukbang* become such a necessity for *honbaps*? How can someone be so attracted to watching a stranger eat on camera? Perhaps it has something to do with the importance of sociality in Korean cuisine: eating has always been something that we've done with family and friends. Eating together makes us feel better; it enables us to share *jeong*, a form of affection, attachment. For people who eat alone, watching someone eat isn't just pure entertainment. We feel comforted and less lonely. *Mukbangers* offer their spectators the company of sharing meals. *Mukbang* has evolved into various genres since it has become one of the main trends on the Internet. Here are some examples.

Zach Choi ASMR

Gongsam Table (이공삼)

Bokyoung

Haet-nym (입짧은 햇님)

MommyTang

Stephanie Soo

Heebab

Fran

ASMR *mukbang*

ASMR stands for Autonomous Sensory Meridian Response, a difficult term that refers to a simple feeling. A sort of goosebumps that usually starts on your scalp and moves down the back of your neck and upper spine. Next time you feel it, concentrate on it: it should be a pleasant and stimulating sensation that helps you feel at ease. ASMR *mukbangers* concentrate on the sound people make when they eat, which should give goosebumps to the spectator. From the sound of slurping noodles to the crunch of fried chicken, ASMR *mukbangers* don't hesitate to eat noisily. They even position powerful microphones as close as possible to their mouths. Here are some names of ASMR *mukbangers* you can find on the Internet:

Zach Choi ASMR
Gongsam Table (이공삼)
Bokyoung

Livestreams and stories on social media

Mukbang began and expanded on the South Korean live streaming platform Afreeca TV. The hosts usually broadcast their videos at lunchtime. But *mukbangers* have increasingly begun using social media to interact more directly with their audience. On YouTube live streams, for example, hosts can interact with the audience in the chat. They describe the taste of the food they're eating, answer questions, and share anecdotes. Here are some *mukbangers* who are famous for their livestreams:

Haet-nym (입짧은 햇님)
MommyTang
Stephanie Soo

Competition

An important aspect of *mukbang* is without a doubt eating large quantities of food. Watching people eat large quantities of food is somehow satisfying, and some people have understood this perfectly, such as:

Heebab
Fran
Banzz

Reality *mukbang*

It's not enough to watch people while they eat, watching them cook is also satisfying. Some types of *mukbangers* claim they're more spontaneous, less contrived ("reality"), and show common people cooking and eating in their homes. Here are some of these programs:

Hamzy
Veronica Wang
KEEMI

Family *mukbangers*

How bittersweet it is to watch families share a meal while we eat alone! And yet for many *honbaps*, watching these types of video is comforting. Some of these families have become so famous that they're perceived as an extension of the *honbap* community. Here are some examples:

Heungsam (흥삼)
B.A.D. Family
Yangco Family Mukbang

Banzz

Hamzy

Veronica Wang

KEEMI

Heungsam (흥삼)

B.A.D. Family

Yangco Family Mukbang

Chapter 3

HONSUL

A Toast to Oneself

나에게 건배

Honsul, like other terms related to *honjok*, is a neologism comprised of the words “alcohol” and “alone.” Although drinking alcohol alone is becoming increasingly common among young Koreans, it remains a new practice and one that is not well understood in Korea. The Korean tradition of drinking is, in fact, the result of a layering of meanings and rules associated with alcohol that have accumulated over centuries. And alcohol is one of the protagonists in the most important rituals of Korean culture, which mark the most significant rites of passage in an individual’s life: maturity, marriage, funerals, and various ancestral rites—there are some for the celebration of longevity and health, others to increase the probability of receiving good news, or to acknowledge a good year of harvests.

As society has transformed in recent centuries—and even more quickly in recent decades—so, too, has Korean drinking culture begun to change. If, in the past, people drank only on specific and more or less sacred days, today alcohol is clearly a drink for the masses, consumed regardless of the occasion and very often with the goal of getting drunk in order to break the ice and forge relationships—especially among colleagues at the end of a long workday. But like other Korean activities, good manners related to the

consumption of alcohol remain ever important. For example, it's considered respectful, both for the pourer and for the drinker, to hold the bottle and the glass with two hands. Alcohol, despite its relative freedom from sacredness, is still considered an activity to share, a cohesive element for group activities. When alcohol is consumed, the needs of the group can become particularly stressful for some people, who therefore become *honsul*; that is, those who prefer to drink alone. *Honsuls*, nonetheless, are considered marginalized in Korean society: drinking alone is perhaps seen as proof that these individuals do not belong to any group.

Actually, in thousands of posts on social media, the hashtag *#honsul* is very often associated with words that cast it as a positive activity and, above all, one that is chosen with freedom and levity by those who practice it. Young *honsuls* often use terms like "romantic," "atmosphere," "self-reward," and "luxury" to indicate that drinking alone is a gesture of self-love—a bit like eating a slice of cake or preparing a cleansing mask for one's face. Even terms such as "simple" and "uncomplicated" can be found: these refer primarily to the simplicity and freedom with which the choice to drink can be made without pressure. There is no need to consider who must drink first and who second, or the quantity of alcohol to drink in order to satisfy the expectations of one's group. Even the term "healing" appears often, which is interesting, as even the owner of a *honsul* pub in Seoul has likened pubs for people who want to drink alone to the psychologist's couch: *honsul* pubs are a healing space. "All of us encounter difficult moments in our lives," the owner of the pub said in an interview with the *Korea Herald*, and "people need a space where they can express their own secrets and feelings." The owner then added that when one is facing a challenging moment, it can

be hard to share it with friends, and this is why many people who frequent pubs alone exploit the opportunity to let off steam with the baristas and strangers alike—a bit like when many of us, at one time or another, have opened up to our hairdresser or some stranger on a train. Learning more about *honsul* may allow us to reflect on the way in which we view—and perhaps judge—people around us who eat and drink alone. The Italian literary critic Emilio Cecchi wrote: "Only one thing is more dismal than someone who eats alone; and that is someone who drinks alone. Someone who eats alone is like an animal at the trough. But a man who drinks alone is like a suicide." It's clear that sometimes drinking alone can represent one of the first symptoms of depression and alcoholism, and it represents precisely that annihilation of the individual that Cecchi refers to. But this is not always the case. Perhaps *honsuls* will help us to understand that someone sitting alone in a pub while reading a book with a glass of wine in hand really doesn't need our pity.

Chapter 3

3.1 Drinking Culture in Korea

한국의 음주문화

HONSUL

South Koreans drink more spirits than anyone else in the world. According to the research institute Euromonitor, if Americans drink three shots of spirits a week and Russians six, South Koreans drink roughly fourteen. South Korea is home to more alcoholics than anywhere else, and the social costs tied to this scourge reach more than twenty billion dollars per year, as estimated by the Ministry of Health and Well-being. But citizens and their government are indifferent to these numbers and seem to express no desire to change their drinking culture.

In South Korea, alcohol is much less costly than it is in other countries, and it's considered an essential part of daily life, especially for those who work. Drinking together with colleagues after work is considered a fundamental practice to alleviate stress and to connect with other people—not so surprising, given that Korea boasts some of the longest and most stressful workdays in the world. Getting drunk is not the goal of drinking marathons among colleagues; rather, drinking is viewed as a way to break the ice and forge ties. The preferred drink of Koreans is soju, a rice-based liqueur very similar to vodka but slightly sweeter.

The result is that in the evening, on the streets of Seoul, one can see increasing number of well-dressed Koreans who have passed out on the street. This type of phenomenon has been documented by the website "Black Out Korea," which was recently shut down, but whose content has been shared on other blogs, where tourists and immigrants published images of Korean men and women passed out on the pavement. Foreigners who sent the photos to the site were surprised and in a certain way disturbed by the normalization of this phenomenon. Koreans no longer seem to notice the umpteenth body passed out on the street.

The consequences of this trend are sometimes tragic. Many people who lie passed out on the streets in the cold risk dying of hypothermia. And even among Koreans, there are those who refuse to identify drunkenness as the main cause of the hypothermia that afflicts many people on winter nights. Both the media and the public often seem to ignore the facts and continue to believe the myth that death by hypothermia is caused by exposure to electric fans. The belief in "death by fan" originated in the 1920s, when a certain skepticism toward this new technology took root, and which persists today in Korea (also, but less so, in Japan) despite the fact that there is no concrete proof to support this idea.

But where should we place *honsuls*, young people who drink alone, in this drinking culture? Within a social culture of drinking, we could imagine those who drink alone as alcoholics, as someone who has totally lost control. But in fact, many *honsuls* often have fewer problems than those who drink socially. Drinking alone, for them, implies not using alcohol as a way to break the ice, and it doesn't expose them to the risk of giving in to the pressures of the group—which is often an incentive to drink more. Drinking alone for some people can certainly mean having a problem. But for others it simply means concentrating more attention on the experience of our tastebuds and on the quality of the drink—and in that case, the risk of a hangover decreases significantly.

Unfortunately, there are even *honsuls* who have drinking problems, but in reality many of them reject low-quality alcohol and prefer to drink more expensive products that are made with high-quality ingredients. We should consider them more as connoisseurs than alcoholics. To respond to this new necessity, E-Mart (the largest discount supermarket chain in the country) has begun to sell young *honsuls* small, individual-sized imported beer, sold at the exorbitant price of fifty thousand won (forty-eight dollars). What's more, many *honsul* influencers often position themselves in front of the camera while drinking a few glasses of beer or a shot of liquor during meals, instead of casting alcohol as an activity on its own. Perhaps this new trend in drinking alone can change the relationship that many young people have with alcohol—and who knows, maybe even help to shed light on the necessity to educate Koreans toward healthier ways of approaching alcohol? For now, we can only hope this will be the case—the phenomenon is so recent that its effects are yet to be seen.

Chapter 3

3.2 Getting Inebriated as Release

자유를 위해 취하다

HONSUL

자유를 위해 취한다

One must always be drunk, said Baudelaire, in order not to be a slave to time. It doesn't matter whether one is drunk on wine, poetry, or virtue. Even the Korean author Park Hong-Soon views drunkenness as a liberation. According to Hong-Soon, in a society in which people must always be aware of their behavior, it's easy to use alcohol as form of escape. In everyday life, in fact, the average citizen is treated like an insignificant being, crushed by a system more powerful than herself. Alcohol, however, can free her from others and their requests, helping her to be in tune with her own needs. Getting intoxicated creates moments in which we can become masters, kings, and gods.

In fact, a young *honsul* wrote in his blog that deviance in drinking is for him trust in himself. His level of self-esteem fluctuates on the basis of how others observe him and how much money he has in his wallet. He often feels anxious, sometimes small. But when he drinks, it's different: faithful to his feelings and to the sensations that he experiences at that exact moment, armed with the impulse that allows him to eliminate from his life the beliefs and judgments that make him feel uncomfortable.

But according to Hong-Soon, in a different society, one in which individual freedom is amply recognized and "unusual" behavior is tolerated, there is no need to get drunk in order to feel in control of ourselves. Perhaps then, even beyond Korea, we can attempt to recognize the reasons why we get intoxicated: is it because once we're drunk, we feel less influenced by the judgment of others? Perhaps we do it to find the courage to say or do those things that otherwise we wouldn't feel free to do while sober? In that case, we can heed Hong-Soon's words and try to find within ourselves—and not in alcohol—the courage to change our societies.

Chapter 3

3.3 Drinking Etiquette

주류 라벨링

HONSUL

주류 라벨링

Drinking, like eating, follows precise rules. When young Koreans come of age and begin to drink alcohol, their elders teach them how to drink with other people. Let's take a look at the most important rules—and remember that when we're alone we can forget them all!

1. The younger person pours the drinks for the older people. Similarly, the person of lower rank must pour the drinks for his or her superiors. This is a clear sign of respect in Korean culture.
2. When you pour alcohol in another person's glass, you must offer it respectfully with two hands, holding the bottle in your right hand and touching your right wrist with the left hand.
3. When someone pours a drink in your glass, hold the glass with both hands. Then lift it, propose a toast with the person who offered it to you, and bring the rim of the glass to your lips.
4. Refusing the first drink, especially if offered by an elder or someone of higher social rank, is a *faux pas* in Korea. It's better to accept, but not finish, what's in your glass. Ultimately, it's normal to wait for the glass to be empty before pouring again. As long as your glass is still partially full, no one can offer you more to drink—so if you don't want to drink too much, be sure always to leave a drop or two in your glass.
5. If you realize that the glass of an elder or someone of higher rank is empty, swiftly offer to pour more. If the person refuses, you can offer to pour more once again. At the third attempt, it's better to stop.
6. It's considered polite to hide your face slightly when you drink with people older than you. Try not to establish visual contact with anyone while you swallow.

Chapter 3

3.4 Soju and K-pop

소주와 케이팝

HONSUL

Honsuls often drink soju, the most prized and widespread alcoholic drink in Korea. This drink is normally consumed in groups, but it's increasingly appreciated alone. It's a distillate made from rice, barley, or wheat, but sometimes tapioca and potato are used; it's similar to a slightly sweet vodka. Adult Koreans drink on average a bottle and a half of soju per week; in 2011, soju produced by the company Jinro was the best-selling spirit in the world. Soju originated in Korea in the thirteenth century, during the Mongol invasion, who had learned new distillation techniques from the Arabs.

Even K-pop stars—that increasingly renowned Korean pop music—have become spokespeople for soju, and in so doing they've made it popular even abroad. Psy, the singer of *Gangnam Style* (whose video is still the most popular on YouTube), told the English newspaper the *Sunday Times* that soju is his best friend. The K-pop singer IU became the face of Chamisul soju in 2014 at just twenty-one years of age, as did Irene of the K-pop girl group Red Velvet, who replaced her in 2018. YouTube is swarming with videos of K-pop band members who pour soju for each other and drink in front of the camera, sometimes competing for who can drink the fastest.

Soju even became a protagonist in the early songs of Jay Park, a hip-hop Korean-American artist on the frontline of the K-pop movement, before he consolidated his position as an independent artist with global success who is now distributed by Jay Z's label, Roc Nation.

A resource for South Korea, soju will be increasingly exported to the West. Not so long ago, soju was unknown in the Western world. In the United States, it was even perceived as a watered-down liqueur that didn't follow the rules of alcoholic distillation. But in recent years, soju has begun to gain ground particularly in America. Soju is high in the ranking of distillates and liquor whose growth is expected to become exponential. On the Internet, there have been 24,000 conversations on soju over the last two years, with an annual growth of 18 percent. To provide a bit of background on these data: it's surpassing the popularity of Japanese sake. Soju is becoming more popular, thanks to word of mouth—people like the sweet and clean taste of soju, which makes it pleasant alone, but also suitable as the basis for cocktails and other drinks. Precisely for its ease of drinking, some people define it as a "dangerous, but fun, alcoholic drink."

Are we ready to drink soju like real Koreans—of course, responsibly—and maybe even like real *honsuls*?

Etiquette

If we drink with Koreans, then it's important to hold the bottle with both hands while pouring the liquor in the glass, as a sign of respect to those present at the table. If we are in the midst of older people or anyone of higher rank, we should also turn and cover our mouth while we drink. If, however, we drink like *honsuls*, that is, alone, then we can avoid following any sort of etiquette.

How to serve soju

Soju is traditionally served straight or on the rocks, in a small glass which has been previously placed in the freezer. It is normally drunk quickly. Some people describe the taste as sweet, clean, and subtle—like coconut ice cream.

Soju-based cocktails

It seems, however, that soju lends itself to being mixed with hundreds of other ingredients, a bit like vodka or gin. Some people mix it with lemon juice, fruit juice, beer, chocolate milk, or seltzer water. There are even those who combine it with a mint-flavored popsicle as it melts. If, however, we prefer to be a modicum more sophisticated, we can try to grate some apples, boil them, and then place them on the ice in the cocktail.

Types of

* ** *** ****

On a first date:

"Is *honsul* your hobby?"

"Yes, I like to drink alone."

"Really? I'm so sorry. You must feel very lonely."

"Excuse me?"

"*Honsuls* are those people who have no one to drink with, right? Just the thought of it makes me feel sad and lonely. Let's drink together from now on!"

"The reason I drink alone is that I don't need to show myself, I don't need to spend additional energy to make others happy. When I drink alone, I do it just for myself, it makes me feel good. I don't think I want to see you anymore."

This conversation is taken from a Korean television series in 2016 titled "Drinking Alone"—in Korean, "Honsul Nam Yeo," which literally means "Men and women who drink alone." Even among Koreans who have more familiarity with the concept, some people still associate the act of drinking alone with the idea of feeling lonely—that is, not having anyone with whom to share that moment. But the reasons why people drink alcohol alone can be varied. Here are several types of *honsul* that can be found in the TV series "Drinking Alone."

BY JADE JEONGSO AN

Honsul

The convenience store type *

In Korea, it's rather normal to purchase alcoholic beverages in convenience stores and drink them in front of the store. Some small supermarkets even have tables and portable chairs that customers can borrow to drink outside. The German version of Korean convenience stores is the Späti. if you're in a hurry and you can't wait to open your favorite bottle of beer until you get home, you could be a convenience store type.

The gourmet **

If you like to pair different types of alcoholic beverages with specific foods, it's probable that you're the gourmet type. As a gourmet, you can't wait to go to a fine restaurant and order beverages to pair with different dishes. What's more, if you eat alone, you might even wear headphones and try to match the perfect music for the situation.

The goodnight type ***

Nowadays, many of us are increasingly busy. Between work obligations, family, and hobbies, at the end of the day, before going to bed, some people decide to drink a glass of wine, beer, or a shot of soju. If you like to end your busy day drinking alone, then you could be the goodnight type.

The influencer ****

The influencer likes to go alone to an excellent wine shop, order a fine wine with a selection of cheeses, and take some pictures of his *honsul* table using the hashtags *#honsul #wine #cheeseplatter*. If you, too, think that drinking alone is more convenient and pleasant, but you nonetheless feel the necessity to share it with someone—posting photos and stories on social media of your solitary drinking—then you could be among the *honsul* influencers.

The HONSUL Club

Situated in the multicultural neighborhood of Itaewon in Seoul, Cakeshop is an underground club that's becoming an icon of youth nightlife. The music ranges from Future House to UK Bass, Garage, Disco, Hip Hop, RnB and other underground genres. I spoke with Samuel Swanson, co-owner of Cakeshop, to discuss some of the changes he's seen in his business following the growth of the *honjok* movement in Korea. Here are some things he had to say to help us understand the essence of *honsul* pubs.

"Increasing numbers of people come here alone. If ours was a traditional pub, where people come exclusively to socialize, then maybe fewer people would come alone. But people come here for the music, and so there's no reason why someone can't come and listen to music alone. Even if you don't come with someone else, you always have the choice of socializing right here.

"If you go to a disco or a pub alone, you're not forced to speak just with your friends all night. Going alone is a liberating experience and, paradoxically, it could also be a heightened social experience.

"Drinking can cause the loss and rediscovery of yourself. Sometimes it's difficult to find oneself in a group with other people. Our club has precisely this aim: it's a place where people can lose themselves and find themselves again alone—but always safely."

BY JADE JEONGSO AN

A DAY *in the* LIFE *of* **Hojoon Kim** 42, male, between a gourmet and an influencer type

Hojoon lives alone in Seoul. His favorite hobby is cooking and sharing his dishes on Instagram. He prefers to cook his food alone; but when he has deadlines and urgent work, he has his meals delivered to his home or he goes to eat in famous restaurants he's become familiar with his gourmet friends. He has many opportunities to drink together with other people, and he loves pairing delicious food with

BY JADE JEONGSO AN

high-quality alcoholic beverages. But when he can, he really likes to spend time—and consume quality drinks—alone.

The first thing he does when he wakes up in the morning is to prepare coffee and have breakfast. For breakfast, Hojoon often reheats what he made the night before—maybe an algae soup, kimchi, and a bit of rice. He arranges them neatly on the table before taking a picture, which he will publish on Instagram with the hashtags *#honbap* and *#emptyingfridge*. The second thing he does during the day is to surf the Internet for ideas of what to eat and drink during the day.

The decision often starts with the alcoholic beverages he already has in the house. If, for example, he has a bottle of Chinese Baijiu, he could look for recipes for chicken dishes that may match the Baijiu. Before every meal, he'll take a picture, and then he'll put down his phone to concentrate on the taste of the food and drinks.

The RANGE of HONSULS

In Korea, it's perfectly normal to drink a bottle of soju, especially in a group and after a day's work. Drinking it alone is a bit more unusual, as this is often viewed as symptomatic of a weakness. But how much we can drink alone—not only in Korea and not only among *honjoks*—why is this socially acceptable? When does one go from being a hardcore *honsul* to a hard drinker?

BY JADE JEONGSO AN

After a long day of work, you enjoy a craft beer or a glass of good wine. You're a light drinker, just what's needed to quench your thirst and feel refreshed. This is the safest and healthiest way to drink alone.

Did you just receive a promotion? Did you finish a project? Some *honsuls* decide to celebrate with a shot of soju. Drinking in these situations usually isn't a problem. Still, if what was once drinking for special occasions becomes more regular, then drinking alone is no longer safe.

"I'm so tired." In this central part of the range, we find *honsuls* who drink too much or regularly and associate drinking with their emotional state. They might begin drinking to sleep better at night, after a hard day, after a breakup or during a crisis period. In these cases, it's more likely that the frequency may gradually increase. People in this group recognize that their habits are getting out of control, and they can make some changes to their routine to bring their alcohol consumption levels into a healthy range.

And then there are *honsuls* who drink alone to get intoxicated. This type of consumption is, actually, not very widespread among *honsuls*, but it may happen that someone's drinking becomes more problematic. People on this side of the range minimize the impact that alcohol has on their lives. And sometimes they end up with negative consequences: they could lose their driver's license or job, or isolate themselves from their social and family network.

혼놀

Chapter 4

HONNOL

Solitary Leisure with Pleasure

HONNOL

혼자 놀기

Honnol in Korean literally means "playing alone," and "playing" in this sense implies a bit like what children do when they're alone: that is, whiling away the time, having fun, exploring the world with curiosity. *Honnol* has become a term to describe any activity practiced alone except for eating and drinking. *Honnol* isn't reserved solely for those who live alone or spend all of their time in isolation: there are some people who feel uncomfortable and restless, or others who get depressed, when they're alone; but even among these people there could be someone who likes to do a few things alone, like grocery shopping, going to the newsstand, working out, or playing an instrument.

For anyone who wants to spend time as a *honnol*, the digital age represents a double-edged sword: on the one hand, it allows people to access a deep well of information—tutorials, e-books, online forums—for any need or interest. On the other hand, however, it can also be a source of constant distraction and comparison with others, which keeps us glued to our screens and can make us feel inadequate as we compare our lives with those of friends or strangers: I read somewhere that we used to look to our friends or colleagues for advice on our hairstyle, whereas now we have to measure up to Jennifer Aniston. Spending time alone with a phone in your hand represents an increasing threat to your mental well-being, precisely because the lives of others—of anyone, not only our friends—are increasingly documented and easily accessible publicly, and they very often publicize positive experiences. For this reason, the Internet has initiated and perpetuated the so-called FOMO (Fear Of Missing Out) phenomenon, which can hinder the time we dedicate to ourselves.

This phenomenon was identified for the first time in 1996 by marketing strategist Dan Herman, who, in 2000, published the first academic paper on this topic in the "Journal of Brand Management." But FOMO was coined by the author Patrick J. McGinnis in 2004, in an editorial published in *The Harbus,* the Harvard Business School publication. FOMO is a form of social anxiety derived by the conviction that others are using their time in more fun, social, or productive ways than we are.

The result is that precious time spent alone could quickly transform itself into an experience of apprehension, inadequacy, boredom, and solitude. *Honnol* time, however, is by definition different: it's intentional time in which we refuse to be passively or negatively influenced by the outside world. It's the moment in which we endeavor to focus attention on an enriching activity—intellectual, physical, or practical—that pleases us and allows us to explore ourselves and the world with enthusiasm and freedom.

In practicing *honnol*, we can regain some of Confucius's original teachings, which, despite what some people may believe, became rigid and traditionalist only through the lens of successive interpretations of his philosophy. Confucius and other Eastern philosophers were, in fact, radical thinkers who revolutionized their societies' conventions and debated how to live a good life and construct a just society. They also went further: they developed a practical philosophy, not as concerned with vast, universal matters as much as posing such modest questions as "How can one's daily life be lived?". Confucius concentrated on the mundane and feasible, in which we can discover much of the *honnol* approach, a way of enacting change through small gestures and activities. According to those who practice *honnol*, trying new experiences—and directing attention to the way in which our body and mind respond to these experiences—has the power to guide us toward new horizons.

Chapter 4

4.1 Looking Outside and Within

자신의 외면과 내면 성찰하기

Honnol doesn't necessarily have to be an activity. It can also mean taking a few minutes to observe something within or outside of ourselves. "I like to spend time alone, even without a reason, just to stop and think. I love my time" wrote a *honjok* boy in response to an article in a blog that asked in what situations people "hated" spending time alone. We're constantly stimulated, and this stimulation makes it increasingly difficult for us to "stop and think." Notifications on our cell phones are like diversions and tranquilizers that can end up dulling our ability to feel the true sense of solitude that Eastern philosophers and thinkers have prescribed for millennia as the pathway to happiness.

"My home is small, but its windows open onto the infinite world," Confucius said. Marcus Aurelius, almost two thousand years ago, warned us not to look for happiness and tranquility somewhere outside of ourselves—perhaps in "a secluded place, in the countryside, at the sea, or in the mountains." For the prepared mind, it's possible at any time to retreat within ourselves or look outside ourselves and find well-being.

The condition of retreating within, of contemplation, must not be confused with isolation. It doesn't require us to be isolated physically or emotionally. It's not a fortification that separates us from the world. It's a place where we can find shelter to cast off the baggage of thoughts and stimulation. Beginning with contemplation can enable us to understand *honnol* not as an activity, but rather as a predisposition. *Honnol* is the curiosity to discover oneself while doing something, without the masks we wear every day, consciously or not, for the outside world.

Chapter 4

4.2 *Jajonshim*

자존심

자존심

"If you have time to complain with the sky, then you have time to take care of yourself," a young Korean writes in his blog. Self-love is highly valued in Korean culture. For Koreans, the word *jajonshim* doesn't only imply self-assurance, it also means a sense of grounding that anyone can achieve despite what happens around us. A group of sociologists from Korea University have written that *jajonshim* gives a moral sense to life. It is pride, dignity, a source of humanity. When we have too much of it, it has a negative connotation: we're irrational, arrogant, stubborn. But when a person has just enough, then she can trust in her own value, and the perception of one's moral value becomes an important social credit in a rigidly hierarchical society like Korea's.

Although *jajonshim* has existed in Korean culture for centuries, it can help us understand the deep meaning of specific *honnol* moments. "We live in times that value what is visible more than what happens inside of us," another Korean boy wrote in his blog. For this reason, when young *honnols* write on their blogs that they make time for solitude in order to "take care of themselves," they imply something that is qualitatively different from the Western ideals of beauty and well-being. Concentrating on grounding oneself requires daily practice, but it doesn't mean simply drinking tea and going to the gym. Grounding oneself is an exercise; it is creating the habit of discovering and cultivating those activities that make us feel good and that increase the perception of our self-worth, despite what society has in store for us.

Chapter 4

4.3 Empathy Service

감성 공감 서비스

감성 공감 서비스

Confucian culture and *honjok* culture conflict over shopping. Korean sociologists Teck Yong Eng and Eun Jim Kim write that Confucian culture, which is the basis of Korean collectivistic culture, encourages customers to forge a relationship of trust with store clerks, based on care, long-term commitment, and shared duty. For this reason, the clerks in Korean stores are trained to be particularly energetic, to ask the customer questions and offer their own opinions in order to be sure they find the right product.

Honsho, on the other hand, means shopping alone, which requires a specific type of empathy, free from contrived pleasantries. Just last year, Lotte Department Store, one of the largest in Korea, decided to become *honsho-friendly*, providing signs or stickers with "*honsho*" written on them, which customers can wear if they want to shop alone without clerks hovering around them. If, in fact, interest on the part of clerks can seem useful and pleasant, sometimes it can be frustrating not to be able to stop and think without being assailed or feeling pushed to buy something that doesn't reflect who we are.

Lotte Department Store gave a name to this initiative: "Emotional empathy service." It may seem like a worthless battle, but the freedom to buy what you want without sensing the influence or judgment of others is no small thing in a society like Korea's (and even elsewhere), in which "lookism"—that is, discrimination based on beauty and style: in other words, appearance—is an integral part of the culture. Imagine, for example, the difficulties for a queer person who wants to try on clothes that don't correspond to their biological sex. In this way, *honsho* is a new manifestation of the *honjok* need to not receive opinions or judgments unless they are requested.

Chapter 4

4.4 *Honjok* Concerts

라이브스트림 콘서트

라이브스트림 콘서트

"A concert works when the musicians and the audience reach a sort of unifying experience," Jim Morrison said, "when the borders that separate people disappear." But is it possible to reach a unifying experience when you're closed in your room? A new way of listening to music collectively, but also virtually, which blurs the border between personal and social listening, is taking root in South Korea as a result of the devastating restrictive measures put in place during the pandemic.

K-pop is at the forefront of this new virtual pioneering. Without performance, in fact, K-pop is transformed, it loses value. So BTS, the most famous K-pop group in the world, after having postponed their tour "Map of the Soul" due to the pandemic, for the first time sold tickets for a live, on-line concert: "Big Bang Con: The Live."

But it wasn't simply a streamed concert. The faces and voices of more than seven thousand people appeared on an enormous mosaic in front of the singers as they performed in an empty arena. This augmented reality enabled fans to interact, taking turns, directly among themselves and with the singers. Certainly, the adrenaline of being just a few hundred meters from your idols was missing, as well as the acoustics of the concert and being surrounded by thousands of people singing at the top of their lungs. It seems, however, that through technology, BTS managed to create a unifying experience, opening a new era in performance culture that transcends the classic format of online streaming. A new concert culture that is, without a doubt, *honjok*.

Chapter 4

4.5 Singing as Release

노래하며 내려놓기

노래하며 내려놓기

Karaoke has been a standard in Korean entertainment since the beginning of the 1990s, when Korea began to import karaoke systems from Japan. In the last 30 years, evenings among friends, classmates, and, above all, colleagues have ended with hours of raucous singing. But it's nothing new for Koreans, who prefer to find release away from the gaze of strangers. This is why they reserve *noraebangs*, literally private "singing rooms" in which even the worst singers can let loose in front of a small circle of friends without the fear of being judged. *Noraebangs* are often found in basements of commercial buildings in neighborhoods known for their nightlife. At the entrance of the *noraebang* karaokes, a cacophony of music and singing in all styles can be heard from the many closed rooms.

It seems, however, that fewer people visit *noraebangs* in groups, perhaps also because of new rules that finally allow workers to refuse requests for socialization from their employers and place a limit of 52 hours on the workweek. A new version of *noraebang* has slowly been evolving and is taking the place of traditional karaokes. Coin *noraebangs*—small karaoke spaces for individuals and couples—are no longer found underground; they are now well lit and decorated in bright colors. Instead of paying an hourly rate, which would be too expensive for individual customers, anyone who visits can pay a per-song rate, a bit like paying for a jukebox. These spaces are becoming increasingly popular among young *honnols*, who frequent them not only to practice singing alone, but also to find distraction from their thoughts and to relieve stress.

Chapter 4

4.6 Solo Travel

혼자 여행

혼자 여행

The book *Why I Travel Alone*, by Katrin Zita, has had particular success among young Koreans. Jiwon Jessica Kim, a Korean girl, was struck by Zita's words and in her blog wrote that traveling alone may seem to many Koreans a terrible way to use one's resources: using money, time, and energy to spend time alone is the apotheosis of sadness and contradiction.

According to Kim, however, young Koreans are increasingly beginning to appreciate solo travel. Traveling alone is a mental state, a method: the state of being constantly alert increases our ability to observe. It also enables us to free ourselves of obstacles and concentrate on what we're interested in doing and seeing. Kim, for example, tells about having visited over thirteen art galleries and museums as a solo traveler in Paris, and about having traveled alone to Hawaii to scuba-dive with manta rays.

Traveling, however, requires humility. Moments of discomfort and disorientation, which are inevitable while traveling, force us to confront our linguistic, cultural, and physical limitations. They put us in our place. If in those moments we have the support of our close group, like friends and family, we are somehow ensconced in our own bubble—with the risk of reinforcing stereotypes and misinterpreting what we're experiencing. But facing those moments alone, surrounded by strangers who belong to another culture, can also be a transformative experience and a catalyst to change the way in which we relate to others. What's more, traveling alone doesn't mean refusing company in any form. Rather, it's a question of setting off without yet knowing your travel mates.

Chapter 4

4.7 Driven by Passion

자신의 열정에 전념하기

"We indulge in our passions in small doses, but spending time alone allows us to pursue them with all our heart," a *honjok* girl wrote in her blog. Sometimes the social context, above all in collectivistic cultures, can paralyze our desire to pursue some passions because they aren't consistent with the image that others have of us. Our societies could demand that the role we carry out in the community represents our main or dominant identity, perhaps the only significant one. This is precisely why the time we spend alone is fundamental: it provides us with a personal lens to explore our interests; it's a space in which we can dedicate ourselves to our passions without having to justify them.

Lane Kim, the young South Korean girl in the TV series "Gilmore Girls," is a perfect example of the clash among different identities that young Koreans face today: Lane loves rock music, but, given her strict upbringing and her mother's religious observance, she can dedicate time to it only when she's closed in her room where, methodically, she hides CDs in the closet, under her mattress, or even under the floorboards. Lane isn't free to be herself outside her bedroom door, but inside she can explore her identity and in time find the courage to be herself even in the outside world. *Honnol* time is time that, like Lane, we can dedicate to our passions away from the judgment of others; it's a true "free time" that allows us to choose our loyalties and identities.

Chapter 4

4.8 Discovering New Worlds

신세계에 눈을 뜨다

Learning new skills is one of the preferred ways of passing time for *honjoks*, and in Korea there is a growing number of ways to learn them within the confines of one's home. The Korean government has created an increasingly solid digital infrastructure and developed an "untact economy": that is, a system that allows people to do anything without interacting with others in the physical world. As we can imagine, this market has grown rapidly with the spread of the COVID-19 pandemic. Here are some examples of skills that would have been impossible to learn alone (and economically) without the Internet, not only in Korea but in many other countries in the world.

Learning a foreign language

An increasing number of programs and apps, like Duolingo and Babbel, but also YouTube, allow us to assimilate grammar, phonetics, and fundamental rules of a language. The app Tandem allows two people who speak different languages to have a conversation and learn the other's language. Of course, the best way to learn a language is to live in a place where we'll be forced to speak and listen to that language 24/7: ultimately, we're destined to be penalized when learning a language until we completely immerse ourselves in the culture that produced it. But the Internet can give us all the tools we need in order to start with a solid base.

Working out and playing sports

Some sports are impossible to practice alone, so it's natural to look for workout buddies to motivate us and with whom to share the physical exertion. But performance anxiety and embarrassment as we learn a new sport—especially at the amateur level and as an adult, and maybe even in a crowded gym—can persuade many of us to stop before we even begin. There can also be other reasons that make getting together with others impossible, like lack of time, money, or our friends' availability. There are, however, some sports that lend themselves particularly well to learning at home through tutorials. For example, you can make a foam ball bounce off the wall to learn how to play volleyball, or purchase a ball attached to a rubber band and a weight to learn how to play tennis. Many people head to the city parks alone to fly a kite, which is considered an official sport in Korea.

Dabbling in foreign cuisine

In the past, we could only turn to books to teach us the main dishes in foreign culinary traditions. Not only that, but we were probably able to learn only dishes of the most well-known and widespread cuisines. The Internet, however, can open up a world of regional variation and even familiar alternatives of the same recipe. We can even use social media to ask strangers in other countries for tips and suggestions.

Learning how to play a musical instrument

Besides online tutorials and courses, the digital world is revolutionizing the processes of learning how to play a musical instrument. For anyone who wants to learn how to play the piano as an amateur, there are apps like Flowkey and Scoove, which enable us to learn how to read a musical score more quickly, and others like Pianu, which show us which keys to press at the right time without even having to learn how to read music.

Learning about works of art

The museum experience is much more enriching then simply looking at artwork on a screen. Museums aren't only for learning; they're spaces for exchange and meeting other people. Inside physical museums, culture and freedom of expression are in the air. But digital initiatives that make art available to everyone online are extremely precious because not only do they help to close the social divide between those who are privileged enough to have access to art and those who are not, but they also enable us to see artwork that otherwise would have been hidden in the vaults for decades. Google Arts & Culture has collaborated with over 2,500 museums and galleries across the world to offer virtual tours and online exhibitions of some of the main institutions in this sector. Among the museums we can digitally "visit" are the Uffizi in Florence, the British Museum in London, New York's MET, the National Gallery of Art in Washington, the Musée d'Orsay in Paris, and even Seoul's National Museum of Modern and Contemporary Art.

Chapter 4

4.9 Connecting with Nature

자연과의 연결 · 산림욕

Salim yok means “bathing in the forest,” and this expression is taken very seriously by Koreans and their government. Taking a bath in the forest means walking in nature with intention: perhaps walking more slowly than usual and paying attention to the different shades of green, to the fragrance of the vegetation, to the sound of twigs breaking under our feet and the wild animals around us. In 2014, the Korean government invested 140 million dollars in the creation of a National Center of “forest healing,” and in 2015 the Korean National Assembly passed a law to promote the well-being of forest areas and the creation of “forest complexes of healing.” These areas are complete with aquatic centers, rehab facilities, and digital detox programs, as well as gardens in which walking barefoot is allowed, grassy areas where aromatic herbs grow, open-air gyms, and more than fifty kilometers of trails.

Schools have even been established in the forests: from preschools to elementary schools, but even specific courses have been held there to address the bullying phenomenon. The state has pledged to create a social assistance plan based on connecting with nature. Together with the birth of new infrastructures dedicated to reinforcing the bond between citizens and the natural environment, a new professional figure has emerged—that of the “instructor of forest-based healing,” who is a combination of tour guide, psychologist, and life coach—which requires a university degree in Korea.

Nature walks are one of the *honnol* activities preferred by many young Koreans, who, as soon as they can, flee the city for a weekend of *salim yok*. In fact, despite the expansion of cities, 82% of Koreans visit forested areas more than once a year, and the phenomenon is growing. An entire sector has emerged around the practice of *salim yok*, founded on the idea that our body and brain have developed for millennia in nature, and, therefore, that a part of us feels at home in nature. Various studies have shown that spending time in the natural environment has a calming effect on our nervous system. A study conducted at the University of Essex, in England, observed that nature walks diminished depression levels as much as 70% in participants. Additionally, some research suggests that just spending time in an environment that reproduces nature images, like photographs and paintings on a wall, has the power to reduce anxiety, blood pressure, and pain. It appears, for example, that post-surgery recovery is faster for patients whose rooms have a view of a garden.

Together with forest bathing, a sector known as "virtual environment therapy" is taking hold. It intends to offer benefits even to people who, for one reason or another, are unable to enjoy life in the open air. The phenomenon of virtual "forest bathing" has already been exported to the United States, where a penal institution in Oregon has carried out experiments on its prisoners. Researchers found that prisoners who spend 40 minutes a week in a room filled with video screens that reproduce nature scenes are calmer than those who work out in a room without videos. In the same way, video games that simulate natural environments in a realistic way, and that allow players to explore the world freely, are becoming increasingly popular. In Firewatch, for example, players can wander along hiking paths of the Shoshone National Forest.

Obviously, sitting and watching images of nature is not the same as being immersed in it, not only for the physical benefits one receives, but also for the pleasure that forests grant to all of our senses, not only our eyes and ears: feeling

the sun and the wind on our skin, touching a rock, smelling flowers. In any case, *salim yok*, whether real or virtual, can help us in moments of isolation, stress, or anxiety, such as those that we've had to face during the pandemic. It's not necessary to take long and dangerous hikes in untamed nature or to join a costly wellness retreat. A few minutes a day spent sitting in a park under a tree, touching the grass and concentrating on the sound or movements of insects and birds around us, or an occasional weekend of camping, could make a difference.

MUST-HAVE

Here are the apps and websites that no *honjok* can do without. Perhaps this list can show us that the needs of *honjoks* are very similar to our own.

Coupang

Coupang.com is the most widespread e-commerce site and app in Korea. Customers can literally choose among millions of products, including food. It currently delivers 3.3 million products a day. "Rocket Delivery" guarantees deliveries the same or the following day.

Kakao Talk

This is a messaging app, also known as "KaTalk," that's used by 93% of smartphone owners in Korea. *Honjoks* can stay in touch with calls and videocalls on the Kakao app, and they can even read the news!

King of Honjok

Honjokking.com is a website and an app much loved by *honjoks*. It offers informative content, suggestions, and even events organized by the community in case a *honjok* wants to go out with one of their kind. This is the perfect tool if you want to find the best *honbap* restaurant or if you want to feel part of a community that understands your challenges and your joys.

BY JADE JEONGSO AN

TECH

Market Kurly

This is a virtual instant food delivery service that allows its users to order high-quality food directly from its website and receive it the following morning.

Netflix and Watcha

Netflix has become the television of our age and generation in the West, and it is gaining ground in South Korea. The platform has invested in producing Korean television series, known as "K-dramas," one-upping established Korean production outfits. If you can't find what you're looking for on Netflix, it can surely be found on Watcha—the main Korean streaming service.

YouTube

YouTube has become a trusted friend of *honjoks*, allowing them to satisfy the need for any type of company: from entertainment, to education, to news.

10000recipes.com

10000recipes.com is another beloved website and app because it offers easy recipes to try at home with few ingredients and guaranteed results.

Types of

*   **   ***   ****   *****

Solo travelers are increasing—and traveling alone is a trend not only in South Korea. According to a poll conducted by Booking.com in 2018, 28% of people from around the world declared that they would like to plan a trip alone. In Korea, there are various types of *honyeojok* (*hon*, from *honja* "alone"; and *yeo*, from *yeohaeng* "voyage"); solitary travelers who used to travel the world alone and who will resume doing so once the pandemic restrictions have been loosened.

Hocance lovers *

Hocance is the Korean version of a "staycation," a Korean neologism that means spending a vacation in a hotel. These travelers love spending time alone in luxurious hotels, ordering room service and taking a hot bath with a glass of champagne. If you feel regenerated after a few days in a hotel, you now have a term to describe this experience!

The planner **

The planner type likes to organize every single move during a trip. Traveling alone means being able to book a large number of guided visits to places on your itinerary—visits that would require hours of debate with friends or your partner. For the planner, efficiency is important: choosing itineraries that facilitate seeing as many tourist attractions as possible and meeting strangers with whom to share some parts of the trip.

The adventurer ✻✻✻

The adventurer is a rather extroverted *honjok*. She loves to spend time with others, but considers it very important to experienc some things alone—if not necessary from time to time. The adventurer is courageous enough to take an intercontinental flight alone. She loves the idea of sleeping in hostels, making new friends and exploring new places independently. She's not afraid of stepping out of her comfort zone, and she often finds herself deviating from established plans as she reacts to what she encounters along the way.

The *inssa* ✻✻✻✻

This term is used in Korean to mean an "insider," a person with whom it's easy to get along and who knows the hottest trends at any given time. *Inssas* know the best restaurants and don't need to wait in line to get into the disco! The dominant trait of *inssas* is a strong presence on social media. If you're an *inssa* and travel alone, then your friends and relatives know they won't miss a minute of your trip between stories and posts!

The *chabak* ✻✻✻✻✻

Cha means "car" in Korean. *Bak* comes from *sukbak*, which means lodging. *Chabak* means camping, and it's a new trend throughout Korea—mainly a consequence of the coronavirus pandemic. Solo campers flee from the city to spend time at peace with themselves and in nature. They can't wait to park at the campsite and prepare a barbecue-for-one while drinking a cold beer and watching the sunset.

LOVE *in the* TIME *of* HONNOL

Not all *honjoks* reject romantic relationships. I had a chat with Eunji, a young Korean woman who works as a journalist in Seoul, who likes to practice *honbap* and *honsul*. She's in a monogamous relationship that's been going on for some time, and we spoke about how she spends her time as a *honjok* despite the fact that she has a partner, and about how her lifestyle has influenced, and will continue to influence, her past and future romantic life.

BY JADE JEONGSO AN

“I’m rather independent and I like eating alone, especially at work. Because my job requires that I speak with many people, I like to unplug and be alone when I eat. I also like drinking (moderately) alone! I have this fantasy of going to a fine wine shop and tasting many types of wine alone. But for now, I drink alone at home.

“I’m very happy with my partner. We are both independent people, so we understand that if one of us isn’t available at a certain time and doesn’t answer a call or a message, then they’re probably busy and we’ll talk later. We never argue for such foolishness.

“Everything began with small things I’d do alone, which made me understand that I could do other things alone, too. For example, in the beginning I used to drink coffee alone in a café. Nothing too difficult. Then I began eating alone in restaurants. In the end I was able to drink soju alone in a pub. The more I realize I can do things alone, the more I feel free. This has allowed me to be less obsessed with how I relate to others. Realizing that I can do things alone has made me feel complete, free and independent in my relationships.

“I don’t think that *honjoks* are lonely people. I’ve never heard a *honjok* say they feel lonely. I also think the fact that people accept each other as individuals is a wonderful phenomenon in our society. But at the same time this phenomenon saddens me, because I fear it can become a social problem, like what’s happening in Japan.”

At this point I've written more on *honjoks*—young Koreans who do more and more things alone—than they have written on themselves. I studied their society, I interviewed them, I spent hundreds of hours on their blogs and their YouTube pages. I spoke at length with sociologists to understand how to interpret this phenomenon. I have, of course, interpreted them through my own culture, my own intellectual tools, and perhaps I have arrived at what I'd like them to represent to me, to us. The challenges of young *honjoks*, however—that is, of anyone who strives for self-determination in a collectivistic society in order not to succumb to the roles assigned to him or her by tradition—are also my own. Perhaps because I'm Italian, and Italians are placed halfway between American individualism and Asian collectivism. Perhaps it's because I'm a woman. Perhaps it's for both of these reasons. As I studied, however, I realized that I became more ambivalent toward this phenomenon.

I had recently read an extract from the book *Together,* by Vivek Murthy, Surgeon General of the United States in the second Obama administration. Murthy, in his role as "physician of the nation," expected above all to find himself dealing with obesity, illnesses tied to tobacco and opioids, mental health, illnesses preventable with vaccines.

But as I toured the United States to hear which issues were the most pressing, it became increasingly clear that the principal issue had never been identified as a health problem. It was solitude, which united, like an invisible thread, many of the most evident problems that physicians were bringing to his attention.

When I interviewed the Korean sociologist Andrew Kim Eungi—who studied the *honjok* phenomenon upon his return to Korea after having spent several years in Canada—I naively asked him whether he thought that one day the *honjok* lifestyle would be exported to the West. He laughed. "Perhaps we could say that Koreans are aligning themselves with the Western lifestyle," he answered. *Honjok* may be the product of a deterritorialization, of rapid access—through the Internet—to foreign lifestyles, desirable for some, but incompatible with lifestyles that surround them. A recurring example: searching for happiness independently of marriage and family ties.

Is *honjok* just another manifestation of a solitude-based epidemic? I wondered in what way it was appropriate to discuss it, or whether I should distance myself from it. In no way did I want this book to become an exhortation of solitude, a glorification of lives modeled on that individualism that swells within us until there's no room for anyone else.

I resorted to what I normally do in these cases: I continued to study, and I realized that despite being part of a global trend, *honjok* had distinctive characteristics that deserved to be understood. I learned, for example, that it's important not to treat it as a twin of other behaviors found in other Asian countries, for example Japanese *hikikomori*, which describes a very different experience: the search for extreme isolation and social reclusion. This condition in Japan is treated as a mental illness, as a socialization problem. It's more difficult to identify with *hikikomoris*. Young *honjoks* are not necessarily recluses or asocial. Every now and then, many of them simply spend Saturday evening at home or they travel alone without feeling ashamed. They don't marry, they live alone, and they don't want to be pitied by anyone for their choices.

It's not by chance that the *honjok* lifestyle is followed more by women and by people who feel they don't measure up to the "Korean good citizen" type: heterosexual, married, and entrenched in the role assigned to them by their gender. Southern Korea continues to be a society in which the unwritten rule of marrying is strong; it is a society based on couples that follows prescriptions that have contributed to gender inequality for centuries. The husband goes to work, the woman is mainly wife and mother. In this context, in addition to women, people who are homosexual, bisexual, and transgender face legal challenges and daily discrimination. The result is that many Koreans prefer not to reveal their own orientation or sexual identity to family members, friends, and colleagues. *Honjok* is a response to this problem, as well; it's a revolution that's finding the courage to emerge.

The subtitle of this book speaks of a South Korean "method" of living happily with oneself. However, *honjok* is a phenomenon full of contradictions, suspended between liberation and alienation, euphoria and distress, revolution and inertia. There exists no official political or social *honjok* manifesto. There are no *honjok* commandments, no list of rules that *honjoks* follow to ensure their happiness, no shared recipe to avoid feeling lonely. In fact, I asked some of the people I interviewed, despite the fact they appreciated spending time alone, whether they ever felt lonely, isolated. What struck me about their answers to this question was their silence, their false starts, the things they said and then denied—the confusion of those who are unable to lose their enthusiasm in the face of the side effects of their own liberation. The "method" this book mentions is an attempt to formulate some conclusions from this phenomenon that can be useful for our lives and societies as well, in particular at this time in which the whole world has been condemned into forced isolation under the pandemic.

I hope this text can be useful in different ways. It can serve as a simple reference book on how to spend time alone, whether we do so voluntarily or not. It may also be a sort of mirror in which we can recognize certain choices that are perhaps considered extravagant in today's society. Perhaps it can even be an invitation to reflect on the fact that there's nothing wrong with wanting to spend time alone, and that we can use that time as a strong antidote against norms and habits that don't reflect who we really are. *Honjok* is an assurance that non-conformism is acceptable, that there's no need to be liked always and by everyone.

But I also hope it can be a catalyst to reflect on the need to build more inclusive societies, to look toward ourselves and others with more kindness and tolerance. Solitude, ultimately, is the perception of a discrepancy between what we want and what we have. Solitude is feeling like we have a more limited social circle than what we'd like, or feeling as if we don't have enough intimacy with the people closest to us. In a tolerant society, people feel less lonely. They can express themselves with others and look at each other with curiosity. Perhaps the *honjok* sensitivity toward others, their lack of judgment on banal and mundane questions, is precisely what we need to build freer communities in which it isn't necessary to close oneself in a room in order to be able to find ourselves.

Silvia Lazzaris

SOURCES

In writing this book, we interviewed young Koreans who practice the *honjok* lifestyle, owners of restaurants and cafes frequented mainly by *honbaps* and *honsuls*, as well as sociologists, journalists, and Korean photographers. Blogs and forums on which young *honjoks* share thoughts, joys, and anxieties about their lifestyle have been a valuable resource for our research. For this reason, rather than publishing a lengthy list of sites, we decided to provide the tools with which to trace our research, and more generally to deepen one's understanding of South Korea, reading words as Koreans intended them.

The most famous search engine in South Korea isn't Google, it's Naver (naver.com), and the most effective translator for Korean is not Google Translate, but rather papago (papago.naver.com), which means "parrot" in Esperanto. Papago offers translations of good quality from English to Korean and vice versa. Once your search terms are translated into Korean, you can copy the Korean characters and paste them into the Naver search engine. To search for information on *honjok*, you can make use of the glossary in this book and the chapter titles, which are in English and Korean. If you have added Papago as an extension on your browser, you can automatically translate the pages of the Naver results to the language of your choice.

The most prominent Korean newspapers are generally a good source to keep yourself informed of the hottest topics in Korea. They often address the issue of increasing single-member families and the birth of the hon-conomy. The *Korea Herald* (koreaherald.com) is the largest English-language newspaper published in South Korea. There you can find national news and in-depth coverage on economics and finance, culture, entertainment, and sports. "Dong-a ilbo" (donga.com) is another important Korean newspaper. Articles can be read using the Papago translator. "Chosun ilbo" (chosun.com) is one of the most influential newspapers in Korea, whose online version can be read in English, Chinese, and Japanese. Reading different newspapers can help you to understand how different sectors of the population interpret, in diametrically opposed ways, the most individualist trends of the new generations. A very interesting article on *honjok* was published in the international magazine *Rest of World* (restofworld.org): it's titled "Tune In, Drop Out," by Ann Babe, a Korean American journalist who lives in Seoul.

Here are some *honjok* pages to follow online:

The Honjok Dot Com site (honjok.me)
The King of Honjok site (honjokking.com)
The Instagram profile @honjokking
The Instagram profile @nicetoneet
The Instagram profile @ninaahn_official
The YouTube page of MommyTang

Interesting reading for those who want to learn more about South Korea:

Essays

Honjok: The Art of Living Alone, by Crystal Tai and Francie Healey. Eddison Books Ltd, 2020.
The Birth of Korean Cool: How One Country Is Conquering the World Through Pop Culture, by Euny Hong. Picador, 2014.
The Burden of the Past: Problems of Historical Perception in Japan-Korea Relations, by Kimura Kan. University of Michigan Press, 2019.
Our Korean Kitchen, by Jordan Bourke and Jejina Pyo. W&N, 2015.
The Korean War, by Max Hastings. Pan; Main Market edition, 2010.

Narrative

Human Acts: A Novel, by Han Kang. Hogarth, 2017.
The Vegetarian, by Han Kang. Hogarth, 2016.
If I Had Your Face, by Frances Cha. Viking, 2020.
The Island of Sea Women, by Lisa See. Simon & Schuster, 2019.
At Dusk, by Hwang Sok-yong. Scribe, 2018.
Drifting House, by Krys Lee. Faber & Faber, 2012.

Happy researching!

My Honjok

What are your favorite *honjok* activities?

- ☐ Eating
- ☐ Drinking
- ☐ Shopping
- ☐ Singing
- ☐ Traveling
- ☐ Learning foreign languages
- ☐ Playing sports
- ☐ Cooking
- ☐ Playing a musical instrument
- ☐ Going to the museum
- ☐ Going to the cinema
- ☐ Taking nature walks
- ☐ Urban trekking
- ☐ Fishing
- ☐ Reading
- ☐ Taking pictures

A) Activities **you like to do** alone

____

____

____

____

____

____

____

B) Activities **you would like to do** more often alone

____

____

____

____

____

____

C) Activities **you could never do** alone

If most of your answers are in the **A** category, then you're a *honjok*!!

If the majority is in category **B**, then you're a *honjok* wanna-be: you're still searching for a balance between the time you spend with others and the time you spend alone.

If almost all of your answers are in **C**, then you're on the other side of the spectrum. And there's nothing wrong with that!

However, if the number of your answers in **A** and **C** is comparable, then you've found your balance between companionship and solo living. Congratulations!

Without Balthazar Pagani, this book wouldn't exist. The trust, the encouragement, the warnings, and even the silence always arrived at the right time!

Francesca Leoneschi and Giovanna Ferraris, your work is like fried food: it makes any text seem good. You are not only the best graphic designers and illustrators in the world, you are also two marvelous companions in adventure. Thanks for making me smile even in the most stressful moments.

Jade Jeongso An: Without you, I never would have known where to look for information on this phenomenon. You've taught me so much. Thanks for your ideas, your guidance, and the enthusiasm with which you joined me on this project.

I thank Professor Andrew Kim Eungi for the patience and kindness with which he answered all of my most naive questions, and for his penetrating analysis of the *honjok* phenomenon.

Sam Oon, a dear friend and diehard K-pop fan: thanks for the long chats on how to write a culturally appropriate book on a phenomenon that belongs to another culture.

To all of my colleagues: Thanks for having ignored the bags under my eyes and my decreased brainpower around imminent deadlines.

I'm grateful to Katie Kropshofer for staying by my side. And to my family, for always believing in me.

And then there's my Austin Argentieri, last but not least. Thanks for already having read the text of this book three or four times. And for all of the times you cooked and cleaned up so that I could write, without ever keeping track. You are my grounding.

Silvia Lazzaris

I would like to thank Silvia Lazzaris, who explored with me the life of *honjoks* from the first day of this project. Writing a book on this topic, so deeply entrenched in my culture, and on this new, fascinating movement in South Korea, has been an important experience. I'm very grateful to Silvia for her lively intuition, editorial help, and continued support in bringing the stories of *honjoks* to life.

A very special thanks goes out to my partner Max, who helped me during the writing of this book; from patiently supporting me while I tried to juggle work and passions, to giving me advice on the rough draft. I really appreciate all of your support!

In the end, I want to thank all of those individuals who kindly spent many hours speaking with me about their personal experiences and the *honjok* phenomenon in general: Dasom Hahn, Eunji Kim, EunKyung Jeong, Nahee Hong, Hyunjoo Baek, Yunjung Cho, Hyomin Kim, Hojoon Kim, Samuel Swanson, and Ludovic Wolff.

Jade Jeongso An

Silvia Lazzaris is a journalist, radio producer, and Italian writer living in England. Her work has been published on national and international media, among which are Corriere della Sera, BBC World Service, Wired UK, Will Media, and Domani. With her work, Silvia has addressed ethical matters tied to the implementation of new technologies in society and the impact of human activity on the environment and communities.

Silvia works as an editor for the platform FoodUnfolded, which is financed by the European Institute of Innovation and Technology and aims to shed light on the impact of individual food choices.

Instagram and Twitter: @silvialazzaris.

Her favorite *honjok* activity: reading philosophy books.

Jade Jeongso An is a social media manager, a translator and writer by day, and an ambitious cook by night. She studied translation and interpretation at Kyung Hee University in Seoul. She became passionate about writing while working freelance for magazines like *Dazed Korea*. With her words, she tries to educate, entertain, and even change the world.

Jade now lives in Berlin, Germany. Passionate about food and sustainability, when she's not writing you can find her veganizing her favorite Korean food or trying to heighten awareness of the climate crisis through different social media accounts, among which is @FaceResponsibility.

Her favorite *honjok* activity: making handmade jewelry.

Francesca Leoneschi is a founding member and creative director of The World of Dot, a graphic design studio based in Milan and specializing in illustration and typography, design and text editing, logo design and branding. Francesca has a multidisciplinary background in architecture, graphic design, and typography. After ten years of experience as senior designer for Arnoldo Mondadori Editore, she joined the Mucca Design studio in New York as art director. Her experience there inspired the decision to create an editorial graphics studio in Milan together with her husband Lacopo Bruno. She has been art director for Rizzoli since 2008. Her studio works for important Italian and foreign editors. In 2019, she published for Abbelville Press the book *Patterns in Art*, together with Silvia Lazzaris and Giovanna Ferraris.

Her favorite *honjok* activity: knitting.

Giovanna Ferraris is a graphic designer and illustrator. She lives and works in Milan. After having studied and worked in Milan and London, in 2010 she joined The World of Dot. At TWoD, Giovanna specialized in cover design, patterns, and vector illustration. Her illustrations have appeared in numerous books among the most important Italian editors. In 2019 she published for Abbelville Press the book *Patterns in Art*, with Francesca Leoneschi and Silvia Lazzaris.

Instagram: @giovanna_ferraris.

Her favorite *honjok* activity: walking in the park.